EXPLORING THE MIND
Man's Search for Mental Health

by Suzanne Loebl
Edited by Sarah R. Riedman

illustrated with photographs

Abelard-Schuman
London
New York·Toronto

Also by Suzanne Loebl:

FIGHTING THE UNSEEN *The Story of Viruses*

© Copyright 1968 by Suzanne Loebl
Library of Congress Catalogue Card Number: 68-8562
Standard Book Number: 200.71589.5

LONDON	NEW YORK	TORONTO
Abelard-Schuman	Abelard-Schuman	Abelard-Schuman
Limited	Limited	Canada Limited
8 King St. WC2	6 West 57th St.	1680 Midland Ave.

Printed in the United States of America

CONTENTS

    Acknowledgments 9
    List of Photographs *11*
1 The Chains Must Come Off! *13*
2 More Chains Come Off *29*
3 Magic and Magnetism *44*
4 The Crusader *54*
5 Hypnotism Becomes Respectable *65*
6 Doctor Charcot at the Salpêtrière *73*
7 Anna O.: The Patient Who Made History *87*
8 The Questioner *93*
9 Dr. Sigmund Freud, Specialist in Nervous Disorders *102*
10 Psychoanalysis Leaves Vienna *115*
11 Shocked to Their Senses *127*
12 The Missing Link *137*
13 Almost Human *148*
14 Chemicals Come to the Rescue *161*
15 Group Therapy *175*
16 "The Time Has Come for a Bold New Approach" *188*
    Bibliography *202*
    Index *203*

"Science is at no moment quite right, but it is seldom quite wrong."
—BERTRAND RUSSELL

*For Judy
who helped*

Acknowledgments

One of the great pleasures in writing EXPLORING THE MIND was to delve freely into the riches of the past. To list all the books and articles used as background material and for inspiration would be an almost impossible task. Sources used include the original scientific writings of those whose story is told here as well as letters, historical accounts, biographies, textbooks, review and magazine articles and obituaries. A selection of the nontechnical material used is presented in the bibliography. My thanks and admiration go to all those on whose work I based mine.

The short quotes from Sigmund Freud's letters and those attributed to him by Ernest Jones are used by permission of Basic Books, Inc., New York; the excerpt on conditions in a London insane asylum on page 32 from A.A. Roback's *History of Psychology and Psychiatry* is used by permission of the Philosophical Library, New York. I would also like to thank Mrs. Minerva Brown for guiding me around Mount Sinai Hospital.

I would like to express my gratitude to the following, who helped by reading and commenting on all or part of the manuscript: Dr. Iago Galdston, Mr. Hayes B. Jacobs, Dr. Aviva Menkes, Mrs. Pearl S. Meyer and Dr. Herbert Morawetz. Though their help cannot be overestimated, I alone am responsible for any possible errors or misinterpretations.

Special thanks also are due to Dr. Sarah R. Riedman, my editor, for her comments and painstaking examination of the material presented.

Finally, I would like to thank my children for serving as a readily available sounding board, and my husband, Ernest, whose lucid criticism and constructive comments have, as always, guided me in my darker moments.

For providing me with photographs and illustrations used in this book (listed below), I would like to thank the following individuals and organizations:

The New York Academy of Medicine for the pictures on pages 14, 15, 20 and 74.

Ars Medica, Smith Kline & French collection, Philadelphia Museum of Art, for the pictures on pages 33, 35, 94, 122, 162 and on jacket.
Abelard-Schuman Ltd. for the picture on page 41.
The American Psychiatric Association for the picture on page 41.

The New York Public Library for the pictures on pages 45 and 49.
The New Jersey State Hospital at Trenton for the pictures on pages 57 and 63.
Editions Masson, Paris, for the drawing on page 81.
Sigmund Freud Copyrights, London, for the pictures on pages 119 and 125.
Smith Kline & French for the picture on page 129.
The Joseph P. Kennedy Jr. Foundation for the pictures on pages 139 and 146.
The University of Wisconsin, Regional Primate Research Center for the pictures on pages 154 and 155.
Ciba Pharmaceutical Company for the pictures on pages 165 and 167.
The Menninger Foundation for the picture on page 181.
The Museum of Modern Art for the frontispiece.
The National Institute of Mental Health for the pictures on pages 176, 178, 190 and 193.
The photographs on pages 25, 27, 77, 85, 100 and 199 were taken by the author.

Suzanne Loebl
New York

PHOTOGRAPHS

Hospital corridor at Saint Rémy, France *Frontispiece*

Pinel unchaining the insane   14

Johann Weyer   15

Philippe Pinel   20

View of the old Salpêtrière   25

Statue at gate of the Salpêtrière   27

Bedlam Hospital, London   33

St. Luke's Hospital, London   35

Benjamin Rush   41

Seal of American Psychiatric Association   41

Franz Anton Mesmer   45

Mesmer assembling patients around magnetic baquet   49

Dorothea Lynde Dix   57

Dix room at New Jersey State Hospital   63

Jean-Martin Charcot   74

Charcot's clinic at the Salpêtrière   77

Charcot dissecting a brain   81

Man with facial paralysis   83

Charcot's private library   85

Stamp honoring Anna O.   91

Sigmund Freud   94

Tablet on wall of Charcot's clinic   100

Sigmund Freud, 1920   119

"The Sleep of Reason Produces Monsters" by Goya   122

Sigmund Freud's consulting room in London   125

"Whirling Cage" by De Pol   129

Ivar Asbjørn Følling   139

Steuben crystal trophy of seraph Raphael   146

Baby monkey with two types of surrogate mothers   154

"Motherless" monkey   155

"The physician curing fantasy" (etching)   162

Rauwolfia serpentina plant   165

Laboratory monkeys   167

Group therapy session   176

Family group therapy   178

Dr. William C. Menninger   181

Picnic area at psychiatric center in San Diego   190

Patient disassembling transmitter (occupational therapy)   193

Modern mental hospital   199

1 THE CHAINS MUST COME OFF!

Johann Weyer: 1515-1588
Philippe Pinel: 1745-1826

How dare we fix the limits which divide what is normal from what borders on a state of illness?

—Philippe Pinel

In a now abandoned lecture hall in the Salpêtrière Hospital in Paris hangs a large dusty oil painting. It seems to be out of place here. There are no beds, bottles, surgical instruments, pajama-clad patients, doctors or nurses. Instead, it appears to be the courtyard of a prison. In the foreground, a short man, carrying a long walking stick, calmly watches a guard removing heavy fetters from a disheveled young woman. Other chained figures are huddled against the wall.

In spite of its subject matter, the painting shows one of medicine's great moments: Philippe Pinel unchaining the mentally ill, in Paris, in the year 1795.

Philippe Pinel unchaining the insane at the Salpêtrière in 1795.

At one time, in antiquity, the mentally ill were treated with kindness and understanding. But a cloud of ignorance had descended upon medicine; during the Middle Ages, when Europe was raked with pestilence, the insane — believed to be possessed by "evil spirits" — fared even worse than the rest of suffering humanity. Insane women were regarded as witches, and the punishment for witchcraft was burning at the stake. Often, those who disputed this interpretation were themselves considered insane, and, therefore, willful accomplices of the devil. In this age of darkness, there were, nevertheless, a few who defied the accepted views of their times, and risked the stake rather than keep their peace. One of the best-known among them was Johann Weyer.

THE CHAINS MUST COME OFF!

He was born in the year 1515, in the small town of Grave on the river Meuse, in what is now Holland. He studied medicine in Germany with the great physician and philosopher, Cornelius Agrippa von Nettesheim, and later completed his education in Paris and Orléans. A keen observer Weyer left descriptions of scurvy (vitamin C deficiency), quartan fever (malaria), influenza, trichinosis and other diseases, but his major interest was the study of mental disorders, and some authorities consider him the father of modern clinical psychiatry.

Johann Weyer

Weyer made many accurate observations on the nature of mental disease, but since he lived during Europe's "Dark Ages," his most important task was to insist that "witches" were just "perplexed, poor women," whose illness stemmed from natural causes.

It was Weyer's good fortune to be appointed private physician to William, Duke of Cleves. The Duke himself suffered from chronic depressions, as did many members of his family. Consequently, he had a deep enough understanding of his own suffering to offer his brave physician, who was so interested in diseases of the mind, full support and protection.

Weyer often accompanied the Duke to his castle in Hambach, in the German Rhineland, and there, while his master hunted deer in the surrounding forests, the physician found time to work on his most famous book: *De Praestigiis Daemonum* or "On the Delusion about Demons." The book took twelve years to complete and was published in 1563.

The long letter, addressed to Duke William, which accompanied the manuscript, testifies to the courage and the humility of the writer:

Of all the misfortunes which the various fanatical and corrupt opinions . . . have brought in our time to Christendom, not the smallest is that which, under the name of witchcraft, is sown as a vicious seed . . . no such great misfortune results as from the . . . opinion that childish old hags, whom one calls witches or sorcerers, can do any harm to men and beasts.

Almost all theologians are silent about this ungodliness! It is tolerated by physicians and ignored by judges burdened with prejudice. Since no matter where I turn, nobody, but nobody takes pity upon humanity, I took it upon myself to deal with this difficult matter, which disgraces our Christian faith. I am not motivated by pride. I know that I know nothing — and my profession leaves me little leisure. I also know that many could do better than I, and my hope is to stimulate them to surpass me, for I would gladly learn from them ...

To you, oh Prince, I dedicate the fruit of my thought. I have been your physician for thirteen years, and though I have heard many opinions concerning witches expressed at your Court, none agrees so much with mine, as your own: that witches can harm no one through the most malicious will or the ugliest of curses, that it is their imagination — inflamed by demons in a way not understandable to us — and the torture of melancholia, which makes them only fancy that they have caused all sorts of evils.

Weyer stayed with Duke William until 1578. Then, during a temporary illness of the Duke, the witch-hunting faction of the Duchy gained the upper hand, and the life of "Weirus Insanus" (Weyer-the-Insane) was in danger.

Countess Anna of Techlenburg, however, offered him refuge. He continued to take a great interest in all theological and medical matters, even investigating such "modern" subjects as the effect of certain plant hallucinogens (substances that produce illusions) on the human mind. He also maintained his medical practice, and was stricken with his final illness at the bedside of one of his patients.

The church in which he was buried is no more, nor is his grave, but part of the long inscription, originally engraved on his tombstone, reads:

> Johann Weyer, scion of a noble family from the Flooded Sea Lands [Low Countries] was well-known here and abroad because of his devotion to God, his compassion, and his great knowledge of the Healing Arts and public affairs . . . As private physician to the Honorable Duke William of Cleve-Jülich he faithfully served God, Sovereign and Fatherland until the end of his life . . . At the age of 72, tired, mourned by his sons Dietrich, Heinrich, Galenus and Johann, and with invincible faith in Christ, he returned his soul to his Maker . . . His body shall rest here until the Day of Resurrection. May he live in Eternity.

Weyer was never able to convince his contemporaries that insanity was an illness, and two more centuries were to pass before humanity would again look upon the mentally ill with compassion. The witch-hunting of the Middle Ages — that which Weyer had fought so valiantly — abated, and the insane were no longer considered a menace by the Church. They were cared for by the State, but their lot did not improve.

At the end of the eighteenth century, many were still chained down, night and day, like wild beasts. They had barely enough room to stretch out on dirty straw mats. Food was a piece of dry bread and some thin gruel. Often it was "served" once a day and had to be eaten immediately, because otherwise the rats would get it.

The insane were frequently kept together with common

THE CHAINS MUST COME OFF!

criminals. They never saw the light of day. Their cells were freezing cold in winter, stifling hot in summer and steeped in filth all the year round. The howling of the hungry echoed along the halls, and whoever had not entered the "hospital" as a raving maniac, became one after he had been there for some time.

Similar conditions prevailed in many parts of Europe. In London, one of the popular Sunday pleasures was to "visit" the insane asylum as one might visit the sideshow at a circus. The admission fee was one penny. Most of London's demented patients were lodged in the Hospital of St. Mary of Bethlehem, or "Bedlam" for short. Later, "bedlam" became synonymous with "insane asylum," and today we use the word to describe utter confusion and disorganization.

One of the first to take up the cause of the insane again was Philippe Pinel. He was born in 1745 in the small French village of St. André, and his father was a physician. His mother died when he was twelve and, being the eldest, he felt responsible for his brothers and sisters.

He was shy, studious and gentle. Often, when he went hunting with his father, instead of shooting, he preferred to sit at the foot of a tree, deeply absorbed in a book and oblivious to all that went on around him. He loved the Greek and Latin classics and mathematics, and this is what he set out to study at the nearby University of Toulouse, at the age of twenty-two.

We do not know when and why Pinel switched from classics and mathematics to medicine. Whatever the reason, he failed to make a living in the small town where he set up his practice, and, in 1778, Pinel decided to try his

Philippe Pinel

luck in the big city of Paris. Since he did not have money for fare, he walked all the way — 300 odd miles.

He took up residence in the Latin Quarter. In the Middle Ages, when the Sorbonne — the University of Paris — was founded, Latin was the language of scholars. The immediate vicinity of the University has been referred to as the Latin Quarter ever since.

Not even in Paris did medicine provide Pinel with a livelihood, and he supported himself by teaching mathematics and translating medical books from English into

THE CHAINS MUST COME OFF!

French. He did not make a fortune, but did acquire some influential friends, who tried to get him appointed as court physician to the king's aunts.

Pinel actually called on the ladies, but once there, he was overcome by shyness, making a poor impression. Possibly the royal aunts preferred a wittier man. Perhaps it was just as well that Pinel failed to obtain the position. The French Revolution broke out in 1789 and in time, Louis XVI, his queen, Marie Antoinette, and members of the royal entourage perished on the guillotine.

Benjamin Franklin, America's first ambassador to France, was not misled by Pinel's shy appearance. Franklin recognized Pinel's kindness, his vast medical knowledge and his diagnostic skill, and tried to persuade the Frenchman to come to the United States, where good doctors were scarce. But Pinel preferred to stay in his homeland.

In 1782, a tragic incident changed Pinel's career. A friend of his, tired and overworked, lost his reason, and one night rushed off into the woods. The next morning he was found dead, half-devoured by wolves, which in those days still roamed the forests around Paris. This needless loss of life saddened Pinel. Medical science, he felt, should be able to help those who suffer mental anguish, just as it restores those who break a leg or have a fever.

It was then that Pinel decided to make insanity his life's work. Compassion was no doubt an important factor in his decision; but more than that, he believed that mental derangement had a physical cause which should be investigated by the methods of natural science.

He studied incessantly, not only his beloved classics but also all the books on mental disease available from Germany and England. Pinel felt that the ancients, who had treated their mentally ill with kindness, had achieved much better results than those who relied only on repeated bloodletting, cold baths and other drastic measures.

In medicine, however, one can never learn enough from books alone. Pinel started to observe mental patients in one of the few private institutions for the well-to-do. There he tried out his new forms of therapy — work, friendliness, patience — to which he referred as "moral treatment." A few years later he was able to apply these ideas on a larger scale.

France was in a period of turmoil. The nobility that had ruled for centuries was displaced by the middle class. During this upheaval, friends of Pinel, who knew of his interest in insanity, became responsible for the administration of the Bicêtre, one of the largest hospitals in Paris. The institution had a section for the insane in which conditions were atrocious; everyone knew that being put there was the equivalent of a death warrant. If anyone could do something for the inmates of the Bicêtre, it was Pinel.

On August 25, 1793, he was appointed to the hospital. The doctor started by visiting his fettered charges in their dank, squalid, unswept cells. He talked to them for hours at a time. As he wrote later: "How was one to distinguish between the exasperation caused by the chains and the symptoms peculiar to the illness?" The chains must come off, he resolved.

The revolutionary government of Paris — the Commune — was a much-feared institution in those days, but Dr. Pinel decided to put his case before them.

At first, he wrote lengthy letters, then he went himself. He had a shy manner, and his gentleness and distinction

THE CHAINS MUST COME OFF!

made him look like a member of the hated aristocracy. He had to face Georges Couthon — president of the Commune — a cripple, unable to walk, embittered by his deformity and drunk with power. But Couthon listened when Pinel pleaded for the freedom of his patients: "I want permission to remove the chains of the insane in my charge. I have observed my patients at length; I have selected fifty I want to release and to whom I want to give the freedom of walking the gardens of the Bicêtre."

Couthon pondered. Was this man honest, or was he sheltering noblemen in his institution whom he now wished to unchain? "Woe to you if you deceive me," he said at last, "and if you hide enemies of the people among your insane. We shall see."

The next day he had himself carried to the Bicêtre to question the insane personally. The cells were unlocked, and a foul, dank stench greeted Couthon. He attempted to talk to the inmates. His questions were answered with grunts, curses and silence.

"Well, citizen, are you mad yourself that you want to unchain these animals?"

And Pinel answered: "Citizen, it is my conviction that these mentally ill are intractable only because they are deprived of fresh air and of their liberty."

"You may do as you please," answered Couthon, "but I am afraid that you are the victim of your own presumptions."

That very day Pinel removed the chains of twelve inmates. The first to be freed was an English officer. He had been there for forty years but nobody knew why he had been committed originally. He was a violent man.

Once, in a fit of rage, he killed one of the guards with his chained hands and since then everybody kept at a safe distance.

Pinel entered his cell alone. "If you promise that you will behave yourself, I am going to have your chains cut," he told the officer.

"I promise," said the man, "but I don't believe you. Everyone is afraid of me."

A guard removed the chains.

At first, the officer could not walk. He had not used his leg muscles for forty years and they refused to function. At last, however, he managed to crawl out to the open air. "Oh, how beautiful," he exclaimed, when he saw the sky and the sun. The man remained outdoors all day, drinking in the light, the air and the sight of flowers. At night, he returned to a cleaner cell, and two years later he was discharged.

One of the next to be freed was a French soldier. Some ten years earlier he had become involved in a drunken brawl. He had insisted that he was a general and attacked everyone who did not salute him according to his rank. Ten years in the Bicêtre was a high price to pay for this fancy. His name was Chevigné. He was strong and well built, and Pinel made him his bodyguard. Soon afterwards, Chevigné repaid Pinel for his kindness. An angry mob, convinced that Pinel was sheltering "enemies of the people," wanted to hang him from the nearest lamppost. Without the intervention of Chevigné, they might have succeeded.

More patients were released and were again able to enjoy the sun, fresh air and beds of their own. For some, however, liberation came too late; they died shortly after being released from their bondage.

THE CHAINS MUST COME OFF!

Though at first the government had opposed Pinel's ideas, it rapidly recognized his success, and in 1795 he was put in charge of the Salpêtrière — the women's hospital of Paris.

Saltpeter is a chemical substance used for the manufacture of gunpowder and, originally, the Salpêtrière had been built as a powder plant on the outskirts of Paris. Previously, gunpowder had been made in the middle of town, and several explosions had rocked the city. By popular request, the king, Louis XIII, in the early seventeenth century had consented to build another gunpowder plant.

Some people say that the king's decision was less motivated by his solicitude for the safety of the citizens of Paris than by his concern for the wines and champagnes

Contemporary view of the old Salpêtrière.

stored in the winegrowers' guildhall, located across the street from the old arsenal. Be that as it may, construction work on the Salpêtrière was started. The arsenal was surrounded by a deep moat and a crenellated wall, with spaces for shooting as in a fort. Its use as a gunpowder plant was not extensive, but the name stuck. In 1656, it was converted to house the poor and the insane of Paris. In time it was to become one of the great hospitals of France, but that was far in the future.

When Pinel took it over, conditions were as bad as they had been in the Bicêtre. His first task was to unchain the poor and wretched creatures who lived within its walls. As at the Bicêtre, patients learned that he was their true friend and were grateful to him forever after.

Though Philippe Pinel is remembered mostly for striking chains off the patients, he was also a great scholar and teacher. He believed that there must be a cause for every disease, whether mental or physical.

It was Pinel who started to keep a detailed record of the symptoms and progress of each patient. This is called a *case history*. Even today, since there are few medical tests with which to "measure" symptoms of mental diseases — as one can, for instance, measure blood pressure — case histories are especially valuable in psychiatry.

Pinel's colleagues, in England and in Germany, searched endlessly for the physical cause of mental diseases. They measured the size of the head, the skull, the intelligence, the appearance of their patients. Then they drew conclusions.

The French doctor felt they were on the wrong track. He wrote:

Statue now standing at the gate of the Salpêtrière.

I leave it to others to decide whether the analysis . . . has added much to our knowledge of mental disturbances. But another analysis which is even more closely related to the study of human understanding is that of the passions, of their undertones, their varying degrees, their violent outbreak, their varied combinations. . . .

Like modern psychiatrists, Pinel knew that emotions play a vital role in mental disease, and he told his students: "Diseases of the spirit must be treated by the spirit."

EXPLORING THE MIND

In 1826, at the age of eighty-one, Philippe Pinel died in his quarters in the Salpêtrière in Paris. He had opened the doors of medicine to the mentally ill, but everything he hoped for had not yet been achieved. Almost two centuries ago he said:

> In medicine there are few topics as fruitful as insanity . . . there are even fewer topics against which there are as many prejudices to be rectified and erroneous thoughts to be destroyed.

These words still ring true today.

2 MORE CHAINS COME OFF

Vincenzo Chiarugi: 1759-1820
William Tuke: 1732-1822
Benjamin Rush: 1745-1802

During the centuries, while medicine turned its back on the sufferers from mental anguish and torment, the understanding of man's soul was left to the poets. They knew well how to translate conflicting feelings of good and evil into tales that seem truer than real life. Thousands of years after they were first told by Homer, the adventures of Ulysses, Orestes, Oedipus, Achilles and the other mythological Greek heroes are still widely enjoyed, and their stories are a constant source of inspiration to modern artists and writers. Shakespeare lived long before it was understood how each person's "inner world" shapes and is shaped by his relations with the world outside, yet the fears, ambitions, loves, doubts, jealousies and conflicts of his characters so accurately mirror the feelings and frustrations we all encounter, that his plays are a timeless record of human striving and suffering.

While Shakespeare wrote about Hamlet, Lear, Othello and Macbeth — all victims of their own passions — Miguel Cervantes in Spain created Don Quixote, the foolish and valiant knight who spent his life battling windmills and lost causes, being forever defeated, cheated and disappointed, yet never willing to forego "striving against the stream." In the story, Don Quixote's steady companion Sancho Panza — the fat and realistic servant — provides his master with the necessities of everyday life. It has been said that Don Quixote and Sancho Panza are really one and the same person, the servant representing the deluded knight's hold on reality, allowing the Knight to survive and live by his lofty ideals. Such a splitting of personality applies to many mentally ill persons, and, to a certain extent, to all of us. Fantasy, dreams and imagination are as necessary a part of man's mind as are caution and a realistic appraisal of every situation.

While Shakespeare and Cervantes were creating drama and fiction, Robert Burton, a dean of Oxford University in England, wrote, in 1621, *The Anatomy of Melancholy*, later called the greatest medical treatise ever written by a layman. In this book, Burton, a depressed melancholic, describes the symptoms of his own illness. He recalls his unhappy childhood and the indifference of his parents — factors that shaped him into a bitter, disappointed, miserable adult.

Burton devotes much time to the exploration of his inner conflicts, and reaches the conclusion that they were the cause of his feelings of jealousy, competitiveness, hostility and aggression. In spite of his own unhappiness, and that of others whom he suspected of "moodiness," Burton also knew that man derives a certain pleasure from sorrow. *The Anatomy of Melancholy* is prefaced by a long poem, the first verse of which reads:

> *When I goe musing all alone,*
> *Thinking of divers things fore-known,*
> *When I build castles in the aire,*
> *Void of sorrow and void of feare,*
> *Pleasing myself with phantaimes sweet,*
> *Me thinkes the time runnes very fleet,*
> *All my joys to this are folly,*
> *Naught so sweet as melancholy.*

The understanding of the poets as well as the isolated cries for compassion of a few reformers — ignored for so long — were finally heeded by mankind during the last decades of the eighteenth century, and the chains fell not only in France but in Italy, England and the faraway United States of America.

In Italy, reforms were initiated by the Grand Duke Pietro Leopoldo of Tuscany. Though a monarch with absolute powers, he shared the spirit of enlightenment of his times, and in 1774 passed the world's first "law for the insane." In his Duchy, mental patients received medical care, and in 1788 the Duke built the Hospital of Bonifacio in Florence, appointing Vincenzo Chiarugi as director.

The mentally ill were Dr. Chiarugi's chief concern. Along with several of his contemporaries, he opposed unreasonable physical restraints and harsh measures. The Italian doctor was aware that emotions played a role in mental disorders, but he felt that physical deterioration of the brain was the major cause of mental illness. Like France's Philippe Pinel (and later America's Benjamin Rush), he believed that:

> It is a supreme duty and medical obligation to respect the insane individual as a person. It is especially necessary for the person who treats the mental patient to gain his confidence and trust. The attitude of doctors and nurses must be authoritative and impressive, but at the same time pleasant and adaptable to the impaired mind of the patient . . . Generally it is better to follow the patient's inclination and give him as many comforts as is advisable from a medical and practical standpoint.

At times, history seems unfair in the way it chooses to distribute its laurels. Whereas Philippe Pinel became an immortal of medicine, and Benjamin Rush is considered the father of American psychiatry, and William Tuke — the British reformer — is remembered as a great humanitarian, Chiarugi, who liberated the insane five years before his French contemporary, has been almost forgotten. Few of his writings have come down to our day and, contrary to Pinel, he had few followers.

In England, as evidenced by the testimony of an eyewitness before the House of Commons, in 1814, the conditions of the mentally ill were abominable:

> In the women's galleries, one of the side rooms contained about ten patients, each chained by one arm or leg to the wall, the chain allowing them merely to stand up by the bench or form fixed to the wall, or to sit down on it. The nakedness of each patient was covered by a

Bedlam Hospital, London, by William Hogarth. In the eighteenth century, Bedlam was one of the sights of London. Note the two well-dressed women, one shielding her eyes from the nude, make-believe king sitting in the alcove.

blanket, made into something like a dressing-gown, but with nothing to fasten it in front. This was the whole covering, the feet being naked. . . . In the men's wing, in the side room, six patients were chained close to the wall, five handcuffed and one locked to the wall by the right arm, as well as by the right leg; he was very noisy; all were naked except as to the blanket-gown or small rug on the shoulders, and without shoes — their nakedness and their mode of confinement gave this room the complete appearance of a dog kennel.

Medical authorities did not concern themselves with the mentally ill, but relief — in a small way — had come in 1791, in the person of Quaker William Tuke, a tea merchant by trade. Tuke was sixty-one years old when he heard of the fate of Hannah Mills, a fellow member of the Society of Friends, who died of brutality and neglect a few days after she had been admitted to the York insane asylum.

To ascertain whether the reported inhumanity existed throughout Britain, William Tuke went to visit St. Luke's Hospital in London, where conditions were said to be much better than in nearby Bedlam. He didn't have to go to Bedlam, as conditions at St. Luke's were so bad that he resolved to found a home that would at least shelter ailing Quakers.

The matter was discussed at several meetings of the Friends. Since, in addition to its inhumanity, the treatment to which the insane were exposed tended to "depress and degrade the mind rather than awaken its slumbering reason or correct its wild hallucinations," it was resolved on the 28th day of the sixth month, 1792, to "provide a retired habitation, with necessary [medical] advice and attendance for Members of our Society, and others in professions with us, who may be in a state of lunacy or so deranged in mind (not idiots) as to require such a provision."

The resolution also specified that "ground be purchased, and a building erected, sufficient to accommodate thirty patients, in an airy situation, and at as short a distance from York as may be . . . that there be a few acres for

St. Luke's Hospital, London, by Thomas Rowlandson (1756-1827) and Augustus Pugin (1762-1832). This hospital was founded in 1751 to supplement the Bedlam Hospital.

cows and garden grounds for the patients to take exercise, when that may be prudent and suitable."

Then, as now, good accommodations for the mentally ill were expensive, and the Quakers devoted a lot of time discussing how their new venture was to be financed and what rates the patients were to pay.

The "York Retreat" was opened in 1796, and from the beginning was true to its name; a shelter for those in need, a place where many could heal their tormented souls and return, strengthened, to their families.

William Tuke, however, did more than found the Retreat; he also instilled in his descendents a special concern for the mentally ill. His children and grandchildren continued to take an active interest in the Retreat, and his great-grandson, Daniel Hack Tuke, was the first member of the family to become a physician and, not surprisingly, a psychiatrist. He was of delicate health and given to dreaming. His father wanted him to become a lawyer, but the boy preferred to collect skulls and compare their shapes and sizes. This interest occupied him even in school where he liked to characterize and study the shape of the heads of his fellow students. As a young child he loved to visit the Retreat and lie under the enormous elms planted by his great-grandfather. In 1848, at the age of twenty-one, he joined the staff as bookkeeper and rapidly became engrossed in the medical books of the library. He left the hospital to return, later, as a full-fledged physician.

Philippe Pinel and William Tuke had become united in their concern for the mentally ill. After their death, the bond they had formed blossomed in the friendship of Daniel Hack Tuke and René Semelaigne, the great-grandnephew of Philippe Pinel. Both men were practicing psychiatrists, making their own contributions to the cause of the mentally ill. They also took great pride in the history of their families, and wrote about the development of psychiatry in Britain and in France. It was a story to which the devotion and courage of their ancestors had contributed richly.

During the first hundred years of their existence, the American colonies depended almost entirely on Europe for their luxuries, ideas and higher education. Gradually, however, they developed an intellectual life of their own. It was a slow beginning and, in 1745, when Benjamin Rush was born, the founding of the first medical school in the United States was still twenty-one years in the future.

MORE CHAINS COME OFF

Having served his apprenticeship with Dr. John Redman, a leading Philadelphia physician, Rush went to study medicine at the University of Edinburgh, in Scotland, one of the great medical centers of the world at that time. After receiving his M.D. degree in September, 1768, Rush visited hospitals and other medical institutions in London. His friend and fellow Philadelphian, Benjamin Franklin, had given him letters of introduction to the leading physicians at the University. These letters opened the doors for Rush in London, and later in Paris, not only in medical circles but also to the intellectual élite in the arts, literature and philosophy.

After a five-month stay in the British capital, where he attended the school of the famous Hunter brothers — anatomists and surgeons — Rush crossed the English Channel to pay his respects to Paris. He was poorly impressed by French medicine, and appalled by the life and manners of the French royalty. The spirit of *Liberté, Egalité, Fraternité*, which was to culminate in the French Revolution some twenty years later, was much more to his liking.

During the summer of 1769, Rush sailed home aboard the ship *Edward*. One of the few Americans of his time to have visited the Old World in person, he was to travel little during the remainder of his life, being content to wage the battle for better medicine and a better world from Philadelphia — the "City of Brotherly Love."

Like the Tuke family in England, Rush's ancestors were mainly Quakers. Young Benjamin had grown up with strong moral convictions. Being a born fighter, a rugged individualist, a gifted speaker and convincing writer, he spent a lifetime fighting for his principles. He was among the first citizens of Philadelphia to take an open stand against slavery; he detested capital punishment; recognized the evils of alcoholism; believed in equal rights and education for women; and gave his support to public schools. But above all, he fought for the freedom of his country, and during the eventful summer of 1776, he proudly affixed his signature to the Declaration of Independence.

When he returned from Europe, in 1769, he had to fight hard to be appointed professor of chemistry at Pennsylvania's recently founded Medical College. Later he was to hold its chair of Professor of the Theory and Practice of Medicine.

Rush was a popular teacher, and his lectures were always well-attended. But being a teacher was not enough to earn a livelihood; he also had to build a private practice. At first, he sought his patients in the slums of the dock area and in the small towns surrounding the city. He felt more at ease there than among the residents of the fashionable homes in downtown Philadelphia. They took offense at his radical ideas, and his well-established colleagues begrudged him their patients. Little by little his fame spread, and in time he became not only the city's leading physician but the most famous doctor of Revolutionary times.

Benjamin Rush's achievements as a physician, teacher, orator, politician and reformer are many, and today his statue stands in the capital of the nation he helped to found. But it was the mentally ill who were his special concern, and, in recognition of his efforts in this field, his profile adorns the seal of the American Psychiatric Association.

It was at his insistence that the Pennsylvania Hospital had a special section set aside for the care of "lunatics." This wing was equipped with pleasant rooms, a heating system and two bathrooms where patients could be given hot and cold showers and baths, because Rush believed that *hydrotherapy* was an important form of treatment.

In 1812, Rush summarized the experiences he had gained in the treatment of the insane in a book called: *Medical Inquiries and Observations Upon the Diseases of the Mind*. This, America's first psychiatric treatise, was to influence the thinking of the New World on this subject for the next seventy-five years. The book discusses mental illness principally from three points of view: description of the symptoms and manifestation of mental illness; investigation of the causes of mental illness; and finally, suitable methods of treatment for each type of mental disorder.

Before describing the many different forms of "partial or general intellectual derangement" man can suffer from, Rush defines the various functions of the mind: understanding, memory, imagination, passions, the principle of faith, will, the moral faculty, conscience and the sense of Deity.

As he proceeds, Rush shows in what manner one or all of these faculties are affected during mental illness. He illustrates each type of derangement by quoting actual case histories seen either by himself or by other physicians, including Pinel. Thus, even in the days of sailing vessels, the exchange of scientific ideas between Europe and the United States was an important part of medical research.

Rush distinguishes between disorders caused by injuries and malformations, and others. In modern terms, the first would include cases of *mental retardation* or *mental deficiency*, and the *senile psychoses*. The term mental retardation applies to children who fail to develop their intellectual capacities to the fullest, either because of a birth defect or because of a brain injury suffered at birth or early in life. Brain injuries can be caused by physical accidents, by unusual complications of an infectious disease, like measles, by high fevers, and by severe malnutrition. Even today many of the causes of mental retardation are still unknown.

Mental disorders caused by physical changes in the brain, either through accidents or as a consequence of other diseases — such as the growth of a tumor — can happen at any age. (Dr. Rush cites paralysis, fever, excessive eating and other causes.) These are most frequently seen in old people who have suffered changes in the blood vessels that supply the brain. Such cases are referred to as *senile psychoses,* or "insanity caused by old age."

Dr. Rush also distinguished between "partial intellectual derangements," which he defined as diseases consisting "in errors of opinion and conduct, upon some one subject only, with soundness of mind upon all, or nearly all, others." Though this category could include almost all of humanity, more specifically it refers to those who suffer from disorders classified as *neuroses.* Neurotic patients are troubled, to the extreme, by feelings of anxiety, fear, inferiority, or depression. They may have difficulties in holding jobs, or irritate those around them, or be incapable of keeping up in school (though equipped with average or superior intelligence), or suffer from numerous imaginary diseases. In spite of all these maladjustments, neurotic patients usually require little or no hospital care.

The major portion of Rush's book is devoted to those suffering from "general intellectual derangements" or, in modern terminology, *psychoses.* Psychotic patients make up the bulk of every mental hospital population. There are many different forms of psychosis, but by far the largest category is comprised of diseases classified as schizophrenic disorders.

Rush believed that insanity, either partial or general, was mainly a disease of the blood vessels of the brain. "Insanity," he wrote, "can stem from physical causes such as malformations, lesions of the brain, tumors, abscesses, water in the brain, epilepsy, certain odors, famine, extremely hot and cold weather, great pain, intestinal worms, measles," and many similar conditions. Also from violent emotions such as: "Joy, terror, love, fear, grief, distress, shame from offended delicacy, defamation, calumny, ridicule, absence from native country, the loss of liberty, property, and beauty, gaming, an inordinate love of praise, domestic tyranny, and lastly — the gratification of every wish of the heart."

Rush's recommended methods of treatment are divided into two categories, those which act: "I. Upon the mind,

Benjamin Rush

Seal of the American Psychiatric Association bearing the likeness of Benjamin Rush.

through the medium of the body"; and, "II. Upon the body, through the medium of the mind."

His direct methods of treatment included bloodletting, purgatives, cold shower baths (sometimes followed by warm), darkness, camphor, Peruvian bark (quinine) and hellebore. The inventive doctor designed a "tranquilizing chair," in which patients were strapped tightly and swung around and around for hours on end. This he believed to have a calming effect on the mind because it "opposes the impetus [flow] of the blood towards the brain, [and] it lessens the muscular action everywhere. . . ."

Rush also believed in what today is termed *occupational therapy*:

> Maniacs of the male sex, in all hospitals, who assist in cutting wood, making fires, and digging in a garden, and the females who are employed in washing, ironing and scrubbing the floors, often recover; while persons whose rank exempts them from performing such services, languish away their lives within the walls of the hospital.

Treatments that "act upon the body through the medium of the mind" included certain forms of *shock treatment* — some as drastic as instilling "the fear of death" in a patient. Rush cited examples in which the study of mathematics, or listening to invigorating tunes helped the deranged regain their senses. He encouraged his patients to write and talk about their illnesses, and felt that the soft voices and kindness of women were particularly suited to the care of the mentally ill.

Understanding and consideration were not restricted, however, to the fair sex. The physician himself must "acquire the obedience and affection of his deranged patient by acts of kindness . . . justice, and a strict regard to truth."

Rush died less than half a year after the publication of his *Inquiries*. He might have felt that not everything advocated in his book would stand the test of time, but he hoped the spirit that guided him would sustain all those who might follow in his footsteps. He expressed that feeling in the concluding paragraph of his book:

> Here the reader and the author must take leave of each other. Before I retire from his sight, I shall only add, if I have not advanced, agreeably to my wishes, the interests of medicine by this work, I hope my labors in the cause of humanity will not be alike unsuccessful; and that the suffering of our fellow creatures, from the causes that have been mentioned, may find sympathy in the bosom, and relief from the kindness, of every person who shall think it worthwhile to read the history of them.

3 MAGIC AND MAGNETISM

Franz Anton Mesmer: 1734-1815

Great discoveries are sometimes made accidentally in the course of research for something entirely different, without the discoverer being aware of the significance of his findings. Columbus set out in search of a new route to the Indies, and he never knew he had discovered a great new continent.

So it was with Franz Anton Mesmer. He stumbled upon a new method of treatment without ever understanding why it worked. In medical history Mesmer is a much-maligned man. Treating his patients in semidarkness, armed with a "magic wand" and using mirrors and magnets, he seemed more like a conjurer than a physician of the eighteenth century.

Mesmer was a contemporary of Philippe Pinel, but these two men, who stand at the gateway of modern psychiatry, could not have been more different. Pinel was shy and retiring; Mesmer loud and flamboyant. Pinel lived in modest quarters at the Salpêtrière in Paris; Mesmer lived in pomp and luxury. Pinel had convictions in keeping with his own times — the Age of Reason — when modern scientific understanding was displacing superstition; Mesmer was kin to the astrologers of the Middle Ages, who believed that the earth is ruled by mysterious forces emanating from the stars. Pinel was convinced that all mental illnesses have physical

Franz Anton Mesmer

causes; Mesmer believed that health can be affected by unseen, ill-defined forces permeating the universe.

Franz Anton Mesmer was born, in 1734, in Iznang, near the shores of the Lake of Constance in Germany. At first, he studied religion, then law, and, finally, decided to become a doctor.

After he had finished his studies, Mesmer married a rich Viennese widow, and they lived in a luxurious mansion set in a big garden. The house was always full of laughter and music, and the great composers of the day were frequent visitors. Young Mozart was a special friend of the family. As soon as he arrived in Vienna, he would rush over to Mesmer's house. There he played on the doctor's most precious possession, a glass harmonica. One of Mozart's early operas, *Bastien and Bastienne*, had its première in Mesmer's little private theater.

Even though he did not practice, Mesmer took a great interest in all the new developments in science and medicine. He was most intrigued when one of his friends, Father Maximilian Hell — a Jesuit priest and court astrologer to Empress Maria Theresa — told him that he had been able to cure people by drawing out their illnesses with magnets.

Magnets had been used in medicine since ancient times. Philippus Aureolus Paracelsus, the famous Swiss physician and alchemist, born in 1493, had great faith in them. According to him: "The magnet can cure a flux from the eyes, the ears, the nose. It can heal discharging sinuses in the limbs, fistulas, cancer, ruptures, jaundice and dropsy." Magnets did seem to possess unique powers. Could they not show the road to a lone navigator on the high seas, and move metal objects as if by magic?

MAGIC AND MAGNETISM

Mesmer was so impressed by Father Hell's reported cure that he asked him for some magnets. He did not have to wait long for an occasion to use them. On July 28, 1774, a friend of the family, Fräulein Franzl Oesterlein, came to visit. She suffered terrible pains and seemed on the point of death. She had seen many physicians, but none could cure her vomiting, earaches and fainting spells.

Since all the previous treatments had failed, Mesmer asked whether she would be willing to be treated with his newly acquired magnets. He put a heart-shaped one on her abdomen and one on each leg. As soon as the magnets were in place, Fräulein Oesterlein had "the strangest sensations," and went into violent convulsions. Then, she calmed down and, for the first time in months, was free of pain. Her symptoms returned in six hours, and Mesmer treated her again. This time the young lady's respite was longer. After several magnetic treatments, she was completely cured.

Mesmer was both puzzled and pleased. He felt that this new method of treatment should be investigated further. More people came to see him, and he treated them with magnets. Feeling better, they went about spreading his glory, but Mesmer continued to be puzzled. What *was* the healing power of these little pieces of metal that conventional medicine could not accomplish? Was it a force that flowed from one magnet to another?

Within a year, the fame of the "magician", who lived in a house on the banks of the Danube, had spread. Patients came to see him from near and far. His magnets were used to cure headaches, earaches, stomachaches, paralysis, rheumatism and all the other ills and pains that plague humans.

Just about then Mesmer made another discovery. He

realized that his magnets had really very little to do with the miraculous cures. He could accomplish as much by stroking the patients with his hands. His touch alone would throw them into the most violent convulsions and contortions.

Though this discovery did not matter much to his patients, it presented Mesmer with a new problem of trying to uncover the source of the mysterious healing force. From then on, until his death at eighty-two, he continued to search for this force. He called it "animal magnetism" and believed it to be a natural force like electricity, for instance.

Mesmer tried in vain to convince the Viennese medical world of the value of his new method of treatment. Doctors came and watched. But the Austrian capital, which 150 years later was to turn a deaf ear to Sigmund Freud and his revolutionary methods of treating "diseases of the nerves," had no use for Mesmer.

In 1778, after the court physicians had convinced the Austrian Empress, Maria Theresa, that Mesmer was a fraud, he packed his belongings and his glass harmonica and went to Paris. There he was received with open arms by fashionable society. This was some ten or eleven years before the French aristocracy was to be swept away by the Revolution. The court of Louis XVI and Marie Antoinette — the Austrian princess — was bored, and any diversion was welcome.

They flocked to Dr. Mesmer's hospital on the Place Vendôme. Here Mesmer had built big, boat-shaped contraptions, which he called *baquets*. These were filled with big iron rods — magnets — bottles of magnetized water and other trappings, more typical of a country fair than of a

Doctor Mesmer assembling his patients around a magnetic baquet.

hospital. Mesmer believed that the healing force — animal magnetism — flowed from person to person, being magnified in each individual. That was why it was better, he felt, to treat a number of patients at the same time.

Upon arrival for a session, the patients would hold hands and form a circle around the *baquet*. Soft music filled the room for an hour or so. Sometimes Mesmer would play on his beloved harmonica. After this prelude the master, clothed in a flowing cape, would approach the circle, staring into one patient's eyes, touching another with a magnetized rod, grasping the hand of a third.

One did not have to wait long for somebody to start a "crisis." Trembling, groaning, moaning, twitching, dancing, screaming and laughing would seize everyone in the group. The more violent the crisis, the greater the curative effects. After a while, order would return, with everybody relaxing and going to sleep. Then, the patients, relieved of aches and pains, drove off in their fancy horse-drawn carriages.

No wonder the medical world was shocked by such goings on! A commission of scientists — including among others, Dr. Guillotin, inventor of the guillotine, Antoine Lavoisier, the founder of modern chemistry, and from the United States, Benjamin Franklin — came to witness Mesmer's sessions of animal magnetism. They could find no evidence of the curative "magnetic fluid." They testified, however, that many patients seemed greatly improved. The press, too, made fun of Dr. Mesmer, and some of the cartoons of the times have come down to us.

Philippe Pinel also visited the *baquets* and reported his impression to a friend, in 1784. Pinel believed mesmerism to be a passing fad, but was not very disapproving:

> I too wanted to be instructed in the secret, to know for myself what it was all about, and I frequented the *baquet* and even magnetized at Dr. [Charles] De[s]lon [one of Mesmer's pupils] for two months . . . I am a little inclined to prescribe to the ladies this charming maneuver of magnetism. As to men, I repulse them harshly and send them to a drugstore.

Yet Mesmer had many supporters who swore that animal magnetism had achieved lasting cures and was superior to conventional medicine. His practice continued to thrive. He was no longer able to treat personally everyone who came to see him, but he had taught his method to many, and mesmerism had spread across France and the world. But by 1789, France had other worries. Mesmer and his most faithful patients — the high and mighty aristocracy — fled the country. He tried to return to Vienna but was not welcome there either, and so he went to live in Switzerland.

Mesmerism, however, was far from dead. One of the many who had learned Mesmer's method was Marquis Maxime de Puységur. The Marquis was not a doctor but a wealthy landowner. He practiced mesmerism, free of charge, among the poor country folk of his village. While following Mesmer's teachings, to the best of his ability, he made some puzzling discoveries about animal magnetism.

Since Mesmer's magnetic fluid could be "stored," the Marquis had "magnetized" several trees on his estate. The patients were then tied to the trees to be bathed by the health-giving fluid, supposedly flowing freely from tree to patient.

Once, when Puységur was treating a young gardener, named Victor, he noticed that the lad seemed to have fallen asleep. According to Mesmer, the patient's cure was effected by the violent crisis induced by animal magnetism, and Victor would certainly not profit from sleeping! Puységur tried to wake him, but to no avail. This was not the ordinary kind of sleep. It resembled that of sleepwalkers, or somnambulists, who were known to perform fantastic feats, like walking on roof edges, in their sleep.

When the Marquis spoke to him, Victor did not wake. Instead, he stood up, as Peységur had asked him to do. Surprised, Puységur asked him to untie himself from the tree, then to jump, walk and run. Victor obliged, but when he woke up he did not have the faintest recollection of what he had done while sleeping.

Marquis Puységur was very much interested. He successfully induced this kind of slumber in others. They also would blindly obey the Marquis' orders, and then fail to remember what happened while they were under the "spell of the magnetic fluid!"

After his tumultuous life in Austria and France, Mesmer spent his last years peacefully in Switzerland. He continued to treat his friends by the method which had made him famous. In 1813, academic recognition finally came his way. The German Academy of Science invited him to Berlin to explain his teachings, but Mesmer declined. The trip would be too much for him. Two years later he died. He had known wealth and poverty, glory and oblivion, praise and ridicule. When he felt death near, he asked that someone play for him on his glass harmonica, the same one Mozart had played on so many years before.

Mesmer is buried in Switzerland. A sundial and a compass adorn his tombstone, fitting symbols for a man who had traveled far into the realm of the unknown, guided by the magic faith of all explorers, hoping to discover a new continent and getting lost in his search.

Mesmer, however, has another unusual memorial. His friend, Mozart, immortalized the sound of his glass harmonica in *The Magic Flute,* an opera beloved and performed all over the world. Every year tens of thousands hear the clear and cheerful tones of Mesmer's instrument, as the magic bells that protect Papageno, the Bird Man, while he reluctantly accompanies his master, Tamino, through the tests of fire, water and silence. And in *Cosi fan Tutte*, another of Mozart's masterpieces, Mesmer's days of glory are recalled in words:

> This is a piece
> Of Mesmer's magnetic stone
> That came first from Germany
> And then won great fame
> In France as well.

4 THE CRUSADER

Dorothea Lynde Dix: 1802-1887

Reforms seldom last forever. The great doctors and humanitarians who had taken up the cause of the mentally ill had died, and it seemed that, half a century later, the battle had to be fought all over again. This time the cause of the insane was taken up by a woman.

Dorothea Lynde Dix was born in Hampden, Maine, in 1802. Her father, a ne'er-do-well, was unable to keep a job very long and moved his family from one New England town to the next. At times, he was beset by a restless, religious zeal, and wrote lengthy sermons. Later in life, Dorothea spoke of these years with bitterness, remarking that, "she never knew childhood." At twelve, the unhappy girl ran away from home and went to Boston to live with her namesake, Grandmother Dix.

The one bright light in Dorothea's early childhood had been her grandfather, Dr. Elijah Dix, who spoiled the little girl on her visits to the ancestral home in Worcester, Massachusetts. From him, some might say, she inherited her ability to push unpopular causes through the legislature. The streets of Worcester, for instance, were lined by shade trees, planted at the insistence of Dr. Dix at a time when forests were being cut down indiscriminately throughout the country. Dorothea's grandfather also saw to it that Worcester and Boston were linked by a decent road — a forerunner of the modern turnpike.

But Dr. Dix had died by the time Dorothea came to live with her grandmother — a staunch, upright woman who believed in God, virtue, hard work and devotion. The young girl had little time for play, and at fourteen, she opened a school of her own. To look the part of the teacher she wore long skirts. She need not have bothered, for her pupils respected their child-teacher. But the school did not prosper; it was closed, and Dorothea continued her studies. She drove herself mercilessly and, in 1821, opened another school.

Miss Dix was not lenient; she demanded perfection of herself and of others. But in the end her pupils appreciated the stern lesson, and many kept up a lifelong friendship with the teacher of their youth.

Much later, when Dorothea Dix had become famous, one of them recalled:

> She was tall and dignified, but stooped somewhat, was very shy in her manner, and colored extremely when addressed. This may surprise you who knew her only in later life, when she was completely self-possessed and reliant . . . She was strict and inflexible in her discipline, which we, her pupils, disliked extremely at the time, but

for which I have been grateful, as I have grown older and found how much I was indebted to that iron will from which it was hopeless to appeal. . . .

That iron will had been with Dorothea Dix since childhood, but her body was weak and frail. It revolted against the overwork, the sleepless nights, the need for self-sacrifice, the harsh New England winters. Miss Dix had always been sickly; in 1836, she was on the point of death. The school was closed, and doctors sent her on a European trip in the hope that a change of scene would cure her. So she journeyed across the grey and stormy Atlantic, but the trip was too much of a strain. Upon arrival in England, she collapsed completely, with tuberculosis.

For the first time in her life, fate was kind to her. Mr. and Mrs. William Rathborn of Liverpool, whom she had just met, took the ailing woman into their home. For eighteen months Dorothea Dix stayed with the Rathborns. She was showered with love and understanding. She, who in the past had only given, now received kindness and care from people who were almost strangers.

When she returned to her homeland, a frail spinster of thirty-six, too weak to practice her teaching profession, Dorothea seemed destined to live the sheltered life of a semi-invalid.

A knock on her door changed all that. A theology student, John T. G. Nichols, had come to see her. He was in charge of the religious instruction held every Sunday morning at the East Cambridge jail, but he felt that he should not teach the twenty women prisoners. Would Miss Dix know anyone who could perform this task?

Dorothea Lynde Dix

Dorothea Dix thought about it for a few moments. "I will take them myself," she said.

Dr. Nichols protested; he knew of her ill health.

"I shall be there next Sunday," was her answer.

When she went, she discovered that not all of her charges were in jail because they had committed a criminal offense. Her "pupils" included some mentally disturbed. She, then, asked the guard to show her the rest of his realm. This confirmed that the jail was used to house the insane, as well, but their cells were much worse than those of other prisoners. They lacked any kind of heat. When she questioned the jailer he only laughed.

"Anyone knows that the insane are insensitive," he said. Based on this assumption, no heat was provided, even during the icy New England winters.

Miss Dix did not argue with him. She enlisted the help of some kind and humanitarian citizens, and, at the age of thirty-nine, began her lifetime work.

After this first descent into the East Cambridge jail, she spent two years traveling back and forth across Massachusetts, visiting jails and almshouses in Danvers, Newton, Lincoln, Concord, Shelburne, and Taunton. Then she returned home and prepared her case for the State legislature.

Fortunately for those whose flag she carried, Miss Dix was endowed not only with the gift of the pen, but also of persuasion.

Thus she addressed the State legislature:

> Gentlemen . . . I shall be obliged with great plainness, to reveal many things revolting to the taste, and from which my woman's nature shrinks with peculiar sensitiveness. But truth is the highest consideration. *I tell what*

I have seen, painful and shocking as the details often are, that from them you may feel more deeply the imperative obligation which lies upon you to prevent . . . continuance of such outrages upon humanity. . . .

I proceed, gentlemen, briefly to call your attention to the *present* state of insane persons confined within this Commonwealth, in *cages, closets, cellars, stalls, pens; chained, naked, beaten with rods,* and *lashed* into obedience.

Danvers: Long before reaching the [alms] house, wild shouts, snatches of rude songs, imprecations and obscene language fell upon the ear.

Groton: There is no window, save an opening half the size of the sash . . . The occupant of this dreary abode is a young man, who has been declared incurably insane. He can move a measured distance in his prison; that is, so far as a strong, heavy chain depending from an iron collar, which invests his neck, permits.

In Shelburne she saw a man confined in a cage; in Newton there was a young woman lunatic holding her child on her arm. Nobody knew the father.

Miss Dix concluded her address with an appeal: "Men of Massachusetts, I beg, I implore, I demand, pity and protection. . . ."

The brief was a bombshell. Some termed it impossible, some said it was full of lies, but indignation at prevailing conditions carried the day. A bill for the immediate relief of the plight of the insane was passed by a large majority of the Senate.

But victory in Massachusetts was not enough for Miss Dix; its adjoining state, Rhode Island, was also to be conquered. Dorothea Dix knew she could not win her fight singlehanded, but she was a master at winning over followers to her cause. When she saw the plight of the insane in Providence, Rhode Island, she realized that the "hospital" had to be enlarged. A large sum of money would be needed, but where was it to come from? She thought of Mr. Cyrus Butler, the richest man in town.

"You'd sooner get milk out of a stone than money from Mr. Butler," she was told.

Dorothea would not be deterred. She went to Mr. Butler's stately mansion and for a while listened to his small talk about the weather. Then, she interrupted him; "Mr. Butler, I wish you to hear what I have to say. I want to bring before you certain facts, involving terrible suffering to your fellow-creatures all around you. Suffering you can relieve."

The rich man listened spellbound to this determined woman from Massachusetts, who knew so well how to blend a pathetic tale with a practical suggestion.

When she finished, he said, "Miss Dix, what do you want me to do?"

"Sir, I want you to give $40,000 toward the enlargement of the insane hospital in this city!"

"Madam, I'll do it," he answered, and Butler Hospital, in Providence, Rhode Island, came into being.

Relieving the suffering of the insane was one thing. Miss Dix knew, though, that to fulfill her mission the mentally ill must also be provided with new forms of treatment administered by trained medical personnel in new, specially equipped hospitals. Such institutions could not be financed by private citizens alone; tax money must help. So, Miss Dix developed new tactics. She carried on her fight through the legislatures of several other states. Her spokesmen were the people who administered the money and made the laws of the land. She personally persuaded the politicians to fight for mental health appropriations in their states.

Today lobbying has become big business. Large sums of money are spent to win support for reforms and unpopular causes. Existing conditions are surveyed, memoranda are written. Highly trained personnel prepare television, newspaper and radio campaigns designed to influence public opinion, and politicians are courted by influential power groups. Dorothea Dix was her own surveyor, and her own public relations expert; she wrote newspaper copy and she spoke to those who were going to present her case to the legislature. New Jersey was her testing ground. After a day's journey over rough roads in a rattling stagecoach, she would meet with twenty or thirty state politicians in her lodging house. They were as easily won over as Mr. Butler had been.

One New Jersey politician, who came convinced that he wanted none of Miss Dix's reforms, left after listening to her for an hour and a half, saying, "Ma'am, I bid you good-night! I do not want, for my part, to hear any more; the others can stay if they want to. *I am convinced;* you've conquered me out and out; I shall vote for the hospital. If you'll come to the House, and talk there as you've done here, no man that isn't a brute can stand you; and so, when a man's convinced that's enough. The Lord bless you!"

When the Act of Authorization for the establishment of the New Jersey State Lunatic Asylum came up for a vote in March, 1845, the bill passed: eighteen ayes, nays none.

Ground was broken in Trenton, New Jersey. A stately hospital, adorned with fifteen turrets, was built. It was surrounded by lawns and gardens, and from its porch one could see the Delaware River.

For four decades, Miss Dix continued her campaign across the nation. She no longer maintained a home of her own, and on her travels stayed with friends, in guest houses, in the hospitals and asylums she had founded. Weather, wind, rough roads, ruffians could not deter her from her missions. Her letters tell of her ceaseless journeys:

I have traveled more than ten thousand miles in the last three years. Have visited 18 State penitentiaries, 300 county jails and houses of correction, more than 500 almshouses and other institutions, besides hospitals and houses of refuge.

From Oneida, New York, she wrote:

Snow two feet deep, thermometer 27° below zero, gas burners easily lighted by the spark transmitted by the fingers. Thus it is not difficult to realize the severity of the cold so often described by Arctic voyagers.

From Prairie du Chien, Wisconsin:

I am writing at a side table in a telegraph office waiting for a boat to La Crosse . . . after which I shall push up the Mississippi to St. Paul.

In 1854 Dorothea Dix returned to Europe for a rest, but even in poor health she could not forget the cause of the

THE CRUSADER

mentally ill. She was the first crusader the New World sent to the Old World. She went to Scotland, the Channel Islands, France, Italy and Greece. In England she put the plight of the insane before the Home Office; in Italy she spoke to the Pope.

Miss Dix traveled the roads and waterways of the earth until she was seventy-nine. In 1881, she went for a rest to the State Asylum at Trenton, "her firstborn child," and lived there for the remainder of her life.

In her room she had a big map on which little crosses marked each new asylum she had been instrumental in

Miss Dix's room at the New Jersey State Hospital at Trenton.

founding or enlarging. The map bore thirty-two crosses. But more important than these crosses were the seeds of compassion she sowed in the hearts and consciences of her fellowmen.

Dorothea Lynde Dix died on July 17, 1887, at the age of eighty-five. She was buried near Boston. Only a few attended her funeral. One of these, informing Miss Dix's English friends of her death, wrote:

> Thus has died and been laid to rest in the most quiet, unostentatious way the most useful and distinguished woman America has yet produced.

5 HYPNOTISM BECOMES RESPECTABLE

>Ambroise Auguste Liébeault: 1823-1904
>Hippolyte-Marie Bernheim: 1840-1919

Mesmer had been wrong in his belief that "animal magnetism" was a mysterious, natural force; nevertheless, he had discovered a curious phenomenon — a new way of reaching the human mind.

After Mesmer's death, "animal magnetism" became almost the exclusive property of the traveling showman. One day James Braid, a well-known English surgeon, was curious enough to attend a performance at which Lafontaine, a French-speaking Swiss, was to demonstrate "animal magnetism" or "mesmerism." Lafontaine selected a young woman from his audience and asked her to join him on the stage. After he had talked to her for awhile in a calm, monotonous voice, she seemed to fall fast asleep.

"A cheap trick if I ever saw one," said Braid. "The girl must be faking."

Lafontaine overheard this unfriendly remark. He called out, in his halting English, "The gentleman says it's all bog. I say it is not bog. There is no bog in it at all. Come up and examine the lady."

Braid obliged. He lifted the girl's eyelids. Her pupils were contracted as in sleep. He inserted a pin under her fingernails; she seemed to feel no pain. Braid was impressed.

That evening, at home, he tried to see whether he, too, could be a "mesmerist." He had no wand or other "magic" implements. Instead, he asked a friend to stare fixedly at the shiny neck of a wine bottle. Within a few minutes his friend's eyes became moist, then he was fast asleep. Braid's wife was the next "guinea pig." When bidden to stare at the family's sugar bowl, she, too, went to sleep.

Braid knew that he possessed no supernatural powers. He also knew that the sugar bowl and the wine bottle were perfectly ordinary objects. Mesmerism was definitely not caused by a "mysterious natural force" streaming from the operator to the subject, but it was not "bog," either. It was an interesting, as yet unexplained, mental process.

Braid called it *hypnotism*, after the Greek word "hypnos" — sleep. This new name for what Mesmer had called "animal magnetism," and others had called "mesmerism," caught on immediately.

From time to time, Braid used hypnotism to perform minor surgery, and, in 1843, he published a book, in which he set forth his theory that hypnotic states were not caused by "magic," but rather by muscle fatigue — the result of a prolonged period of concentration.

Braid was not the first English doctor to use hypnotism in surgery. James Esdaile had performed 161 painless surgical operations in India — on patients under hypnosis — resulting in a loss of only eight as compared with fifty patients who usually died. And Dr. John Elliotson, a true medical pioneer — who introduced into England the newly invented French stethoscope — had ruined his medical reputation trying to make hypnotism respectable.

The failure of all these men to convince their colleagues of the usefulness of hypnotism is difficult to grasp, since chemical anesthetics had not yet been discovered. The agonized cries of the patients undergoing operations reverberated in the halls of hospitals, and the struggles of those trying to escape the knife made surgery almost impossible.

It was in France, and not in England, that hypnotism flowered for the second time. It emerged from the garden of an unknown country doctor, Ambroise Liébeault.

Dr. Liébeault had a typical country practice in Nancy, a middle-sized town in the northeastern part of France. He attended to all the needs of his patients: delivered babies, set fractures, performed minor surgery, ministered to rheumatism, colds, sore throats and stomach pains.

In 1848, as a medical student, Liébeault had read about Mesmer's work. In 1860, he started to use hypnotism to treat those patients who, in his opinion, might benefit from it. Since hypnotism was not a tried and true form of medicine, Liébeault felt he should not charge for treatments with this new method, and he had no trouble finding volunteers.

Knowing the thriftiness of French peasants, he would tell them; "If you wish me to treat you with drugs I will do so, but you will have to pay me as before. But if you allow me to hypnotize you I will do it for nothing."

Whether it was the inducement of free treatment or the

new method used, Dr. Liébeault's fame spread. Patients in and around Nancy flocked to see the *bon père* Liébeault, and waited until it was their turn to be admitted to his "clinic" — two simple rooms tucked away in the corner of his garden.

Liébeault treated a few patients at a time. In a soothing voice, he told them to shut their eyes and go to sleep. Sometimes, he held the patient's eyelids closed for a few seconds, saying: "You are sleeping as soundly as if you were in your own bed. When you wake up your pain will have disappeared. Feeling will come back to your limbs, your strength will increase, you will be hungry."

And many of Liébeault's patients did walk away stronger and healthier, full of hope and renewed faith.

The French doctor knew it was his words and not hypnotism that did the trick. He *suggested* to his patients that they were well and often it worked — at least for awhile. In thirty-four years, Liébeault treated some 12,000 persons.

The power of sleep and suggestion, for medical purposes, had been recognized, on and off, since ancient times. In Greece, during the fourth century B.C., large temples were erected to Aesculapius, the god of medicine. The sick flocked to these temples for a health-giving ritual. They bathed, paid homage to Aesculapius, prayed and, finally, lay down on the temple floors to slumber. At night, when all was dark and quiet, the god himself — probably impersonated by a priest — would appear. He would restore health by kissing, touching, caressing and stroking the sick. Numerous gifts, still found in various temple ruins, bear witness to the gratitude of those who walked away — cured.

HYPNOTISM BECOMES RESPECTABLE

Many centuries later, the English kings, starting with the reign of Edward the Confessor, were alleged to have had the power to remove illness from their subjects simply by the laying on of their hands.

In 1864, a few years after Liébeault introduced hypnotism in his clinic, he published his findings in a book with the imposing title: *Sleep and Similar States, Examined Especially From the Point of View of the Effect of the Mind on the Body*. It is said that only one copy of this book was sold. Liébeault would probably have been completely forgotten, were it not for the fact that one day he treated a patient of the famous Dr. Hippolyte Bernheim, one of the most fashionable doctors of Nancy. For six years this patient had suffered from sciatica — a very painful nerve inflammation. Having gone from doctor to doctor, in despair, he came to see Liébeault. After a few hypnotic sessions, he walked away cured.

Dr. Bernheim, who had treated this patient for six months without avail, heard of Liébeault's success. Before that Bernheim had not taken his local colleague very seriously; the incident aroused his curiosity and he went to call on the "country doctor." Later, Liébeault was to recall how much he was flattered by the first visit of his distinguished colleague.

At first, Bernheim was skeptical of the older man's methods, but he, too, returned to the little garden and his disbelief rapidly changed into admiration. Eventually, Liébeault and Bernheim became friends and collaborators for the rest of their lives.

In 1884, Bernheim published a book on hypnotism entitled *Suggestion and Its Application as a Therapy*. The book was a success, and Nancy rapidly became a center of study for psychiatrists and neurologists, who were constantly seeking effective ways of treating their patients.

Bernheim kept careful medical records of everyone who consulted him. Within four years, he had used the new suggestion therapy on 5,000 patients, of whom, according to Bernheim, 85 per cent could be hypnotized. Those who did not respond were often persons with serious mental disturbances, suffering from what we refer to now as severe "neurotic and psychotic disorders."

Today, one hundred years after Liébeault settled in Nancy, hypnotism is still poorly understood. Though brain waves indicate that hypnosis and sleep are two distinct states there are nevertheless outward similarities. When people talk in their sleep, which is a common occurrence, they seem to make perfect sense. Yet, when asked about it the next morning, they haven't the faintest recollection of what they said and do not even know that they talked. A hypnotized subject resembles a sleepwalker or sleeptalker in that he also does not remember what he said or did during hypnosis.

Suggestion is basic to hypnotism, and relaxation makes a person more susceptible to suggestion. This is why "talking sleep" is the most prevalent way of inducing hypnosis, though Mesmer, the Marquis de Puységur and Dr. Braid used other means to achieve the same end.

Hypnotic sleep varies in depth and not everyone can reach a *trance* state. In fact, ten per cent of all subjects fail to enter into the early stages of hypnosis. Whether there are personality traits that distinguish a "good" from a "poor" subject has not yet been settled scientifically. But experienced hypnotists must have a knack for picking promising candidates. Otherwise the traveling showman, who amuses his audience by singling out one person from a crowd, would not be so successful. Watching a hypnotized subject perform is awe-inspiring. At the mere suggestion of the hypnotist, he will pet nonexisting dogs, run away from fearful tigers, climb chairs — believing them to be mountains — or go through the motions of diving into water, if he is told that it is time for a swim.

When the performance is over, the hypnotist will "wake" his subject as he put him to sleep, by suggesting that he is to awaken. Nobody, however, needs to worry about a hypnotist who might forget the "magic word." After awhile, hypnotic sleep changes, quite naturally, into ordinary sleep.

Hypnotism can unearth knowledge in a person of which he is completely unaware. One subject, under hypnosis, spoke flawless, classical Greek, even though she had never studied it. After a lot of detective work, it was discovered that when she was a small child, her mother took her along when she went to clean house for an old Greek professor. The professor was in the habit of pacing up and down in his living room and reciting Greek texts.

One of the most interesting aspects of hypnotism is the phenomenon of "posthypnotic suggestion." When awakened, persons will do things that have been suggested to them while they were under hypnosis. If told that the next day, at 3:00 P.M. sharp, they will go and visit their grandmother, they will feel a sudden urge to see the old lady and, at the appropriate time, will ring her doorbell, completely unaware of the fact that someone else sent them on the errand.

Liébeault and Bernheim made use of posthypnotic suggestion and, when awakened, their patients would continue to feel healthy and strong.

Together, the two men from Nancy had become world-famous. Until the end of his life Liébeault had remained a kind, modest and unassuming man who spoke of his lifetime work as "the contribution of a single brick to the edifice many were trying to build."

Dr. Bernheim was more aggressive. He discussed hypnotism and its medical applications in scientific journals and books, and even dared to cross swords with Dr. Jean-Martin Charcot, who was then the world's unchallenged authority on diseases of the nervous system.

6 DOCTOR CHARCOT AT THE SALPÊTRIÈRE

Jean-Martin Charcot: 1825-1893

During the lifetime of Jean-Martin Charcot, born in Paris in 1825, medicine and technology grew at an unprecedented rate. Louis Pasteur discovered the nature of infectious diseases, and demolished forever the theory of the spontaneous generation of life. Claude Bernard put experimental physiology on a firm footing. Anesthesia and antisepsis helped to make surgery bearable and relatively safe. The telegraph was invented, and the first telegraphic message flashed from Washington to Baltimore on May 24, 1844. Europe and America were linked by transatlantic cable in 1866. Ten years later the first successful telephone was developed. It was in this atmosphere of "firsts" that Jean-Martin Charcot laid the foundations of neurology, the science of the nervous system — the internal communication system of living creatures.

The Charcots lived in the Rue Faubourg Poissonière, a

busy street in the middle of Paris. Monsieur Charcot was a carriage builder by trade, and his products were sought after by Paris society. Jean-Martin, the second of four sons, was a quiet child. He liked to read and study; he did not talk much but was curious about many things, and he loved to sketch people, landscapes, buildings — everything he saw.

Jean-Martin Charcot

When time came for the Charcot sons to choose professions, it is said that Monsieur Charcot decided for them. Since he was not wealthy enough to educate all of them, he gave the carriage trade to Martin, the eldest. Emile was destined for the Army, Eugène for the Navy, and Jean-Martin, who always had his nose in a book or a pencil in his hand, was to be sent to school. His father left it up to him to decide whether he would become a doctor or an artist.

Jean-Martin chose medicine, but sketching and art remained a lifelong hobby. Later he collected art and art books. The walls of his study were lined with heavy wooden bookcases, and medieval sculptures greeted visitors in the entrance hall of his house.

At the age of nineteen, Charcot graduated from the Lycée Bonaparte, and entered the University of Paris for his medical education. Though his family lived in Paris, he moved to his own rooms in the Latin Quarter, where many other students lived. Life was cheerful. Students got together in sidewalk cafés and endlessly discussed politics, philosophy and science, as French students are wont to do. Not everybody talked, though. Some, including Charcot, preferred to listen. He wore a small mustache in those days. He was thin and pale, and his long black hair was tossed back. Typical of an artist, he remembered what he had seen and, back in his room, he would sketch, from memory, some of those who had struck his fancy: a dandy, a Bohemian with long hair and a small beret; a peasant from the country, bewildered by the fast pace of Paris. Several of these sketches hang in the Salpêtrière in Paris.

Charcot spent his entire life working and teaching at the Salpêtrière. As a medical student, he frequented the large stone buildings, passing the statue of Philippe Pinel which stood in front of the gate. The wards were a wilderness of sick, paralyzed, trembling old women, but their ills fascinated Charcot, and he resolved to "come back and stay."

University appointments were hard to come by. The candidates had to pass a highly competitive medical examination, and the one who presented the best thesis received the appointment. Much depended on how forcefully the chosen problem was presented, and Charcot was never much of a talker.

He failed the competition in 1857. He tried again in 1860. The subject to be discussed this time was "intestinal hemorrhages." Finally only two candidates remained — Charcot and a now-forgotten opponent, who had made a brilliant presentation.

Fortunately, Charcot was better at arguing a case than at making a speech. He tore to shreds the brilliant presentation of his opponent. He also showed his own great knowledge of French and foreign medical literature, and the jury was impressed. Charcot was appointed and the Salpêtrière remained the center of his professional activities.

In Charcot's own words: "The great asylum holds a population of 5,000 persons, among whom are to be counted a large number who have been admitted for life as incurables; patients of all ages, affected by chronic diseases of all kinds, but particularly by diseases of the nervous system . . . We are, in other words, in possession of a sort of museum of living pathology of which the resources are great." For the next forty years Charcot would sift, catalogue, sort and classify this living museum.

For instance, Charcot believed and proved that many

Charcot's clinic at the Salpêtrière.

tremors, speech disorders, convulsions and paralysis, affecting those in his charge, were due to damage and deterioration of the nervous system.

By then it was known that nerves carry "messages" from and to the brain. (The vasomotor nerves, which regulate the blood circulation, had just been discovered by Claude Bernard.) It was shown that injuries to specific parts of the brain cause specific disorders — such as loss of speech, paralysis of one side of the body, loss of memory or impairment of the ability to read. Little was known, however, about diseases caused by the malfunctioning of the nervous system, in the absence of a known injury. This was the task Charcot tackled.

He had learned from his friend Claude Bernard that changes in the composition of the body fluids often furnish a clue to diseases. Since the Salpêtrière lacked a laboratory where chemical analysis could be performed, Charcot's first act was to install one in an abandoned kitchen. There he also examined the brains of the patients who had died. He would then compare the postmortem findings with the case histories previously recorded. This is how he learned about the relationship between changes in the brain and the symptoms he observed in his patients.

Blessed with the keen, observant eye of an artist — so useful to a scientist — he endlessly scrutinized his patients. He had them walk up and down in his little office in the Salpêtrière. He discovered that certain diseases of the nervous system caused people to limp in a very characteristic manner. He became expert at imitating the walk, or special twitch, in a patient and, often while lecturing, he would demonstrate the limp typical of a particular disease.

Other nervous disorders caused tremors. In some diseases, these increased when the patient attempted to perform a specific task, such as picking up a pencil. In other disorders, the tremors were most pronounced during muscular inaction and disappeared or decreased when the patient concentrated on a particular voluntary movement. Since tremors were often slight, and changes in intensity difficult to observe, Charcot decided to magnify the visibility of the tremor by attaching long white feathers to the fingers of his patients. Then he asked them to perform simple tasks. Would the tremors increase or decrease?

In time Charcot distinguished a whole class of nervous

disorders: multiple sclerosis, lateral sclerosis, locomotor ataxia and others.

In spite of all the progress medical science has made since Charcot's days, disorders of the nervous system are still difficult to diagnose. Most of us give little thought to the manner in which we walk, yet each person has a very characteristic gait. The gait is often one of the first things which changes, when the nerves controlling the appropriate muscles do not operate properly. Today, a hundred years after Charcot, a group of scientists at New York University are again studying the gait in the hope of using it as a diagnostic test to distinguish various disorders of the nervous system.

Charcot did not work in the obscurity of a private practice. At the Salpêtrière, he was king. Nothing was done without his approval. As one of his friends said, "A medical student who knew that Charcot was against him might as well forget the whole thing and become a fish peddler." Charcot was greatly feared at home, also, but his devoted wife was the one who knew best how to talk to him, and often Charcot's colleagues would beg her to speak to the master in their behalf.

In 1870, war broke out between France and Germany. Napoleon III had brought his nation to the brink of ruin, and, in 1871, the Prussian armies stood on the threshold of Paris. Charcot sent his family to England but he remained in the French capital, and went to his hospital daily to take care of patients stricken with typhoid and yellow fever.

In 1872, Charcot was made Professor of Pathological Anatomy and later he occupied the chair of Neurology, created especially for him — the first of its kind anywhere in the world.

In 1883, he was elected to the Academy of Sciences. In his acceptance speech, he stated his belief that without a solid scientific basis, medicine would perish.

> I believe that the practice of medicine does not have a real autonomy, but that it lives on borrowed discoveries and applications; and without a continuous scientific renovation it will soon become decadent.

At the Academy, Charcot had the opportunity to defend his great contemporary, Louis Pasteur, who was under attack by some for his antirabies vaccine.

Charcot lived with his wife and their son and daughter in a large house with a beautiful garden on the outskirts of Paris. He had few intimate friends. Because of his love for animals, the house was full of dogs of all sizes; but the special pet was a small South American monkey, usually seated in a child's high chair next to Charcot at the dinner table.

Later in his career, Charcot became interested in hysteria. Today hysteria is considered to be a psychoneurosis — a disease that takes many forms and manifests itself in a wide variety of symptoms. Hysteric patients may have wild temper outbursts, laughing or crying fits. They may exaggerate their pains or aches, and actually develop sensory disturbances: choking sensation, dim vision, hallucinations. Sometimes, they develop spasms, convulsions and even paralysis. The causes for hysteria are even more varied than its symptoms. The name of the disease comes from

Doctor Charcot dissecting a brain.

the Greek word for *womb,* and, as the name suggests, hysteria was believed to be a disease of women only.

But Charcot showed that males, too, can be hysteric. Without being aware of it, hysteric patients imitate real physical symptoms such as a stiff leg, a paralyzed arm, a running nose or an epileptic fit. Because of his great knowledge of nervous diseases, Charcot could distinguish between paralysis caused by physical nerve damage and one due to hysteria. If paralysis is the result of a physical malfunctioning of the brain, it follows a definite pattern and increases in severity with distance from the brain. A man suffering from paralysis may be able to bend his knee but be incapable of wiggling his toes.

Hysterical paralysis does not follow such a pattern. Instead of the entire limb, a knee or a hand may be all that is affected. The patient may be able to wiggle his toes even though the rest of the leg appears paralyzed. Like Liébeault and Bernheim, Charcot used hypnotism to treat the ill. Charcot, however, believed that only a hysteric could be hypnotized, and that the ability to be hypnotized was, in itself, a disease symptom — one that shows an organic weakness of the nervous system. In this belief Charcot was completely wrong, because Liébeault and Bernheim proved that many people who were not hysterics could be hypnotized.

Charcot's views on the nature of hysteria and on hypnosis were not among his most important contributions to psychiatry. His lasting influence lay elsewhere. He was a great teacher and his students were the leading neurologists, psychologists and psychiatrists of the next generation.

His Tuesday lectures at the Salpêtrière, where he presented and discussed his cases, were famous. They were attended not only by physicians from all over the world, but also by many famous writers, artists and laymen. His lectures covered various diseases of the nervous system, old age (geriatrics), and later on, hysteria cases. These were treated, in public, with hypnosis, and this made the method of treatment more acceptable. Not since Mesmer's days had hypnotism attracted such an audience. Charcot's *Leçons du Mardi,* collected in a book, became one of the great texts of neurology.

Man with facial paralysis (1462-1467) by Nicolas Gerhaert de Leyde. PHOTO: MUSEE DE L'OEUVRE NOTRE-DAME DE STRASBOURG

Art remained Charcot's hobby throughout his life. He traveled widely all over Europe, visiting its churches and museums. Once, in Venice, he was struck by the facial expression of one of the devilish figures carved in stone on the façade of a church. The figure had protruding eyes and a long thick tongue hanging from its mouth. It was fearful to behold.

Charcot, the great physician of the nervous system, recognized a strong resemblance to a patient he had seen some weeks ago at the Salpêtrière. He, too, had had the same distorted expression and a heavy tongue hanging from the corner of his mouth. Charcot took another look at the "damned" and "possessed" which were chiseled in stone on the churches' façades. He found more when he looked at paintings and books. Many of those who had been considered possessed by the devil had the bearing of persons afflicted by disorders of the nervous system. Charcot, together with a collaborator, published these findings in a book, with illustrations, called *Demoniacs in Art*. In this work, Charcot combined the two great passions of his life: art and medicine.

Madame Charcot was worried about her husband's health. He had been suffering from heart trouble for some time, and she felt that a vacation might help. In the summer of 1893, Charcot accompanied by two favorite students, set out for Burgundy, a part of France famous for its wine and its art. On August 15 the party visited the beautiful Romanesque church in Vézelay, richly decorated with medieval sculptures.

When the guard unlocked the gate of the church, Charcot pointed to a hole in the wall, near the entrance. "This recess was for the possessed," he said. "From there they could not even see the altar!"

The vacation did not help Charcot recover his health; he died in Burgundy the day after the visit to Vézelay. His coffin was brought back to the Salpêtrière, and placed in the great octagonal chapel whose dome can be seen across

Charcot's private library, now exhibited at the Salpêtrière.

Paris. The old women patients of the hospital filed past the casket — some walking, some hobbling on crutches and some carried on stretchers — to pay tribute to the man who had devoted his life to the study and aid of "the damned."

His students, in the Old World and the New, collected money for a bronze statue of Charcot in flowing academic robes. This memorial, which stood for more than four decades at the entrance gate of the Salpêtrière, is no more. In 1942, it was destroyed by the Nazis, occupying Paris.

But Charcot's work lives on. As the famous neurologist, Joseph Babinski, said more than thirty years after his teacher's death: "To take from neurology all the discoveries made by Charcot would be to render it unrecognizable. Indeed, not a single day passes in a neurologic service that we do not use some of the notions he introduced; his thinking is always with us . . . By his genius and diligence he has served well not only his country but also the whole of humanity."

7 ANNA O.: THE PATIENT WHO MADE HISTORY

Joseph Breuer: 1842-1925

Our story once more shifts to Vienna, the city on the Danube where Mesmer first had used his magnets to cure Fräulein Oesterlein. Again the patient was a young lady, who in psychiatric history came to be known as "Anna O."

Anna was pretty, vivacious and very, very bright. At the end of the last century, however, upper-class Viennese families believed that the place for women — no matter how gifted — was in the home. Anna was not sent to college and spent most of her day learning how to become an accomplished *hausfrau*. While she embroidered and sewed, her thoughts were lost in the "never-never" land of daydreams or, as she called it, "her private theatre." She was kind and considerate and, when old enough, she derived great pleasure from helping others, who were less fortunate. She liked to take up the cause of the weak — man or beast. Even when she was so sick that she hardly ate, she tackled her huge Newfoundland dog who was fighting with a small cat.

In July, 1880, this pleasant but hardly eventful life changed. Anna's father became gravely ill. He was to die ten months later. Anna, then twenty-one, and her mother nursed him, the daughter usually taking the night shift. Anna loved her father very much. She was distraught by his illness, and the physical strain of nursing was an added tax on her own health. Sometimes she dozed off at her patient's bedside.

Her father did not improve, and after a few months Anna took ill. At first she had a stubborn, hacking cough. Her head hurt, and her neck and legs became partially paralyzed. Her right arm was stiff and insensitive, but she could wiggle her fingers. Her eyes played tricks on her. She had double vision and squinted. At times she could not hear when spoken to. She, who had always been so articulate and clever, now had trouble uttering the simplest sentences. In time she forgot her native tongue — German — and conversed in English only.

Her mother consulted Dr. Joseph Breuer, a noted Viennese physician. The doctor diagnosed his patient's condition as hysteria — a disease to which Dr. Charcot in Paris had devoted considerable time. Dr. Breuer treated Anna for eighteen months, often coming to see her twice a day. It was most unusual for a doctor to spend so much time with an individual patient — a hysterical one to boot. But, during these many months, the doctor and his patient stumbled upon a curious, novel method of treatment: *catharsis* (derived from the Greek word to cleanse), from which psychoanalysis was to grow.

When Dr. Breuer first saw Anna, she was bedridden.

Her day followed a curious pattern. In the morning she acted like a naughty, irresponsible child, throwing pillows, tearing off buttons and being abusive. It was easy to see that something was frightening her; she saw black, slimy snakes and fearful monsters. Later in the day, she napped, and at sunset she would sink into a deep sleep closely resembling the hypnotic state induced by Liébeault and Bernheim for treatment of their patients. Anna called this sleep her "clouds." Finally, she would awake, her mind clear and unclouded, ready to spend a peaceful evening sewing, writing and drawing. At 4 A.M., she would go to bed.

Dr. Breuer had been coming to see his patient toward the evening. Once, when he was bending over the sick girl, he could hear her mutter, "Tormented, tormented."

"What torments you, Anna?" Breuer asked.

To his surprise she started to tell him of the snakes and monsters she had seen that morning. At first, her words came slowly and with difficulty but, after some encouragement, she spoke more coherently. She remembered her German, and proceeded to tell long, sad fairy tales like those of Hans Christian Andersen.

This "talking cure" or "chimney sweeping," as Anna called these strange exchanges with Breuer, became an important part of her day. When, for some reason, the doctor could not come, Anna would spend a restless night and insist on telling him *two* stories the next evening.

By Christmas 1881, Anna had been sick for a whole year. It had become clear to Breuer that she was living in two worlds at once: the world of 1881, which she shared with those around her, and the world of a year earlier, when she had been nursing her father.

That this was the case could be verified by a diary kept by Anna's mother. It also became clear from Anna's conduct. After her father's death, the family had moved to another house. Anna, reliving her past, would forget about her new room. When she wanted to go out through the door, she bumped into the stove, which stood where the door had been in the old room.

Gradually Anna's treatment took another turn. When she was lost in her "clouds," she would start talking about events which had happened at the time her many weird symptoms first appeared.

She spoke of sitting at her father's bedside on one occasion, when her eyes had filled with tears. The sick man had asked for the time, but Anna could not answer at once, as the tears had made the numerals on her watch appear blurred. She had to squint and take a very close look before she was able to see. Since then, her eyes had played tricks on her. After she told Breuer this story her vision returned to normal! Using this method over a period of time, Breuer was able to relieve his patient of her suffering. This "miraculous cure" astonished the doctor and patient alike. Nothing like it had ever been reported in the medical textbooks.

Anna's evening "clouds" did not last long enough for the exploration of all her troubles, especially since it quickly became apparent to Breuer that she could not be hurried along the path of remembrance. The doctor then spent even more time with Anna. Whenever possible, he came in the morning, and induced hypnotic sleep artificially. After Anna was hypnotized, he would ask her to concentrate on one of her symptoms: her faulty hearing; her need to speak English. When had her arm first felt numb?

ANNA O.: THE PATIENT WHO MADE HISTORY

Little by little, the thread of lost memories was uncovered. Her arm had grown numb the evening she had dozed off at her father's bedside. In her half-sleep she had seen a black snake slither toward the bed. She wanted to chase it, but her right arm would not move; it had fallen asleep. In her terror she tried praying, but she could find no words. Finally she thought of an English nursery rhyme. Since then she prayed and thought in that language.

After eighteen months of treatment, Anna had much improved. She was resuming a more normal existence. But she had also become very attached to the physician who took such excellent care of her.

Breuer had entered a whole new and unexplored field of medicine. He did not understand the nature of the memories he had unlocked, and when he realized how much Anna depended on him, he became frightened. He

West German commemorative stamp honoring Bertha Pappenheim (Anna O.), benefactor of humanity.

believed Anna to be well. With almost no warning, he left for a vacation in Venice.

Anna thus abruptly lost the support of the man to whom she had *transferred* some of her feelings for her father. She became ill again and was put in a sanatorium. But she must have had a great will to get well, and in the end she recovered.

Anna O.'s real name was Bertha Pappenheimer. Even when she was bedridden and distraught, she had attempted to help others. As soon as she was well again, she became Germany's first social worker. She attained fame in her own right and, after World War II, Germany issued a commemorative stamp bearing her likeness. Though she was unusually attractive she never married, but spent her life fighting for women's rights. She also ventured to Russia, Poland and Rumania several times to rescue children whose parents had perished in pogroms against Jews.

Breuer and his patient did not understand how catharsis, the method of treatment they had developed, worked. Another Viennese physician, a friend of Breuer's, was to demonstrate that the forces operating in Anna's illness as well as in her treatment were part of a more general phenomenon.

Actually the case of Anna O. would not even have been recorded had not Breuer's friend, Dr. Sigmund Freud, seen in this one case the seed of a method by which to treat the mentally ill — a method which Philippe Pinel had perhaps visualized one hundred years earlier when he said: "Diseases of the spirit must be treated by the spirit."

8 THE QUESTIONER

Sigmund Freud: 1856-1939

Canst thou not minister to a mind diseased
Pluck from the memory a rooted sorrow
Raze out the written troubles of the brain . . . ?
— MACBETH

Sigmund Freud was born on May 6, 1856, in Freiberg, a small town in Moravia — then an Austrian province. His father, Jacob Freud, was a cloth manufacturer. The industrialization of this trade had ruined his business and he had a hard time making ends meet. In the hope of bettering their financial situation, the Freuds moved first to Leipzig, Germany, and then, in 1859, to Vienna, the Austrian capital.

Amalie Freud was Jacob's second wife and less than half his age. Sigmund, her firstborn, was unquestionably her favorite. For him nothing was too good, and his five sisters and infant brother soon learned to defer to the eldest. In

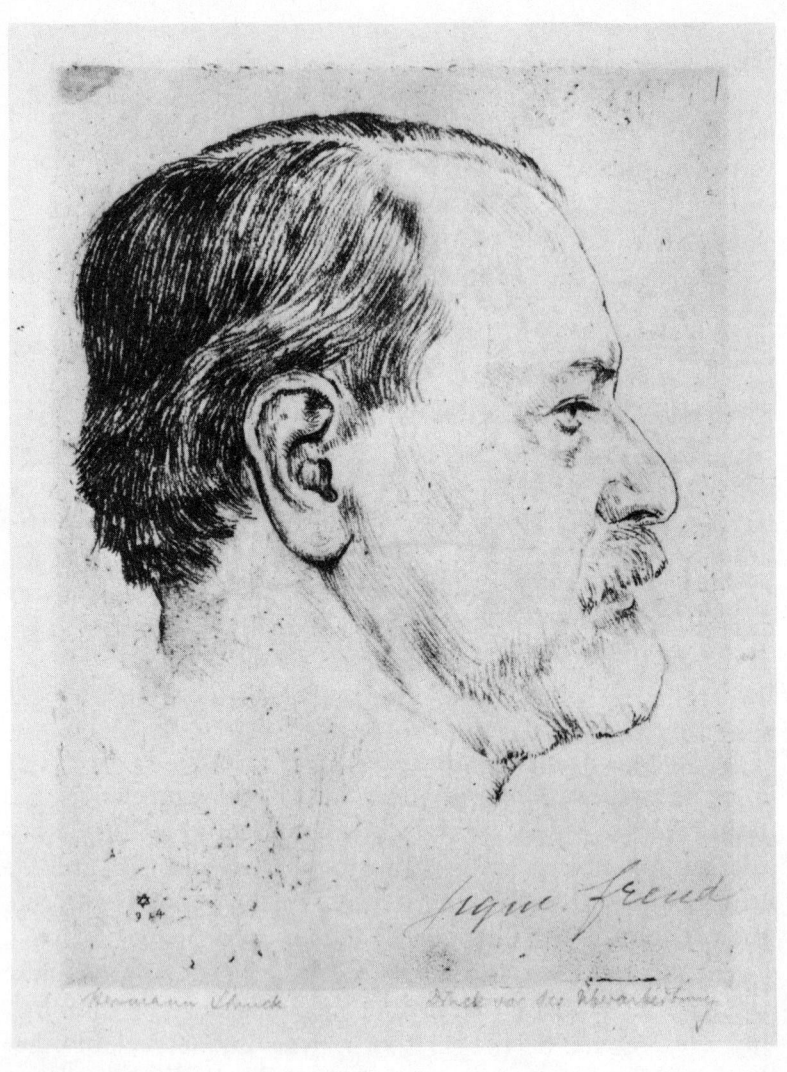

Sigmund Freud by Hermann Struck.

Vienna, even though the family's income was small and the Freuds lived in close quarters, Sigmund had a small room of his own, illuminated by the only oil lamp in the apartment. Amalie believed that her son was destined to have a great future, and his mother's conviction sustained Freud during the lonely years he spent searching for new ways of helping the mentally ill.

The Freuds were Jewish. For two thousand years the Jews had been persecuted in many parts of Europe and Asia. To escape their fate they had moved from land to land. But even where they were tolerated, discrimination was seldom absent, and it affected the Jews' choice of profession, their rights to ownership and where they could live. In the cities they resided in ghettos; in rural areas they were forbidden to own land. They were often excluded from the army, as well as certain professions and the affairs of state. Many earned their livelihood as craftsmen, shopkeepers and peddlers, but even in extreme poverty, the Jews remained true to their appellation: "the people of the book." The most respected members of their communities were the rabbis and rabbinical scholars.

When the Freuds arrived in Vienna, a number of the old restrictions had been lifted. However, century-old discrimination cannot be wiped out overnight, and though Sigmund Freud could attend the University, nevertheless, his life was to be shaped by anti-Semitism. Sigmund entered the Sperl Gymnasium in Vienna when he was ten. He was a good student, and graduated with the highest honors. He handled his native German with elegance, and though the books he wrote later dealt with scientific subjects, they were written beautifully enough to earn their author the Goethe Prize, Germany's greatest literary award. He also had an exceptional gift for learning foreign languages, being completely at home in Latin, Greek, French and English.

At seventeen, Freud entered the University of Vienna. He could have studied anything he wanted, but practical considerations limited his choice to medicine and law, since the practice of either profession for a Jew was the equivalent of "being in business for himself." Even though Freud never showed much liking for being a practicing physician, he chose to study medicine, hoping that it might be a back door to scientific research. This chance came three years later, in 1876, when he went to work for Professor Ernst Bruecke, one of the foremost physiologists of his day.

Professor Bruecke, Director of the Institute of Physiology at the University, was impressed by young Freud's keen mind, his skillful hands, his enthusiasm and his seriousness of purpose. Freud worked in the physiology laboratory for the next five years. At his professor's suggestion, he started to investigate the microscopic structure of the spinal cord nerve cells of a certain type of fish, and in time made some important contributions to the knowledge of nerve tissue. In July, 1878, Professor Bruecke presented these findings at the Austrian Academy of Science.

In 1881, Freud received his medical degree. He was twenty-five, and in no hurry to set up a practice. He preferred to continue his work at the Institute of Physiology. By that time, he held the position of demonstrator, with some teaching responsibilities and, in 1882, hoped to become an assistant to Professor Bruecke. In fact, Freud dreamed that perhaps one day he would succeed Bruecke but, because of the prevailing anti-Semitism, Freud did not receive the assistantship, and there was no future for him in physiology at the University. This was a great blow to Freud's finances. All these years, he had been supported by his father, whose small savings had dwindled so that the young student had to borrow money. He was determined to become financially independent, especially since he planned to get married.

In April, 1882, he had met Martha Bernays, and it had been love at first sight. By August they had become engaged and were to be married the following year, as soon as Freud received the expected appointment. But Freud was denied the coveted position, and Professor Bruecke advised him to abandon the idea of an academic career and find another way of earning a living. To enter private medical practice was the obvious solution, but for this he needed the usual hospital internship and residency.

When the Bernays family heard of the delay this would entail, they urged Martha to break the engagement. She refused. Martha's father had died in 1879, and in 1883, Mrs. Bernays decided to return with her daughters to her native Germany. Perhaps there Martha would forget her brilliant but poverty-stricken fiancé. The separation only increased the lovers' ardor, and for four years they wrote to each other daily, Freud's letters totalling about 1,500!

Deeply disappointed, Freud resigned from Professor Bruecke's laboratory, to join the staff of the General Hospital in Vienna for his required clinical experience. In 1882, he started rotating among the different hospital services: first surgery, then, in turn, internal medicine, psychiatry, dermatology and nervous diseases. He had continued to live with his parents, but in May of 1883 he moved to the hospital, where the routines were apparently not to his liking. From his letters to Martha we gather that he was overworked, attending patients in the wards, reading his way through mountains of books and papers, feeling, sometimes, that "these were the right conditions to help one survive a long separation." At other times he had "to fight against the sensation of being a monk in his cell. . . . Strange theories, diagnostics, formulas have moved into brain accommodations, most of which have been standing empty . . . the whole of medicine is becoming familiar and fluid to me; here bacteria live, sometimes turning green, sometimes blue; there come the remedies for cholera. . . . When a letter from you arrives the whole dream fades, life enters my cell."

To make Martha's presence more real, and also to remind himself constantly of the end in view, he had asked her to embroider two wall panels for his room. One taken from Voltaire's Candide:

TO WORK WITHOUT REASONING

The other, by St. Augustine, read:

WHEN IN DOUBT, ABSTAIN

Freud returned to experimental laboratory work, this time under the direction of the chief of the psychiatric section of the hospital, Dr. Theodor Meynert, considered by some to be the greatest brain anatomist of his times.

Under his guidance, Freud became completely engrossed in research, and wrote Martha: "I am at the moment tempted by the desire to solve the riddle of the structure of the brain; I think brain anatomy is the only legitimate rival you have or ever will have."

But he resisted the temptation of devoting his entire

professional life to anatomy, for this would mean waiting again for a University appointment which might not materialize. As planned, he prepared himself for private practice, intending to specialize in the diseases of the nervous system. He did, however, wish to remain associated with the University and, on the basis of his anatomical research, sponsored mainly by his old friend, and former chief, Ernst Bruecke, he was finally appointed Privatdozent (a nonfaculty appointment peculiar to Germany and Austria), in 1885.

That same year he applied also for a traveling grant awarded by the state to one of the graduating residents. Again on the recommendation of Ernst Bruecke, he was given the award and planned to use it to study with Professor Charcot in Paris. Joy radiates from his letter to Martha, whom he was going to visit on his way to France:

Princess, my little Princess,
Oh, how wonderful it will be! I am coming with money and staying a long time and bringing something beautiful for you and then go to Paris and become a great scholar and then come back to Vienna with a huge, enormous halo, and then we soon will get married, and I will cure all the incurable nervous cases. . . .

After his summer holiday Freud took the train for Paris. For nine months he was to absorb knowledge at the Salpêtrière under the guidance of the great French master. Every Tuesday Freud went to the small, shabby hospital auditorium to attend Charcot's famous *Leçons du Mardi*. A marble plaque on the wall of the lecture hall reminds today's visitor of the months Freud spent there.

Freud was spellbound by Charcot. Later he was to write:

As a teacher Charcot was perfectly fascinating; each of his lectures was a little masterpiece in construction and composition, perfect in style and so impressive that the words spoken echoed in one's ears, and the subject demonstrated remained before one's eyes for the rest of the day.

At the Salpêtrière, Freud continued his anatomical research, but it was soon abandoned, essentially never to be resumed, and he devoted himself entirely to clinical cases. In Paris he concentrated on the study of hysteria, particularly the paralysis that accompanies certain cases. He soon learned to recognize the paralysis due to hysteria rather than to a damaged or injured nervous system. What caused

"Here Sigmund Freud attended Charcot's lectures from 1885 to 1886." Commemorative tablet on wall of Charcot's clinic at the Salpêtrière in Paris.

this hysterical paralysis? His teacher had no answer, except that it must be due to a trauma that *could not be seen.*

During the latter half of his life, Freud was to search for this "unseen" trauma, the elusive cause of what is broadly called *functional* mental illness.

While in Paris, Freud asked Charcot's permission to translate into German his *Third Series of Lectures on the Diseases of the Nervous System.* With his gift for languages Freud finished the translation so rapidly that the German edition appeared four months before the French original. Familiarity with the French master's work increased Freud's admiration of it, and he fully shared Charcot's belief that in science one has "to stare at the facts over and over again until they speak." When Freud returned to Vienna he asked Martha to embroider another wall panel with one of Charcot's favorite sayings:

ONE MUST HAVE FAITH

In Vienna Freud took up his duties as director of a neurological clinic in the new Institute for Children's Diseases, a post secured before he left for France. At last he felt qualified to start a private practice for the treatment of diseases of the nervous system. He was not yet the "great scholar" he had envisioned in his letter to his beloved; and while he was far from being able to cure all the incurable "nervous" patients, at least Martha and he could get married.

9 DR. SIGMUND FREUD, SPECIALIST IN NERVOUS DISORDERS

In Freud's time, doctors specializing in diseases of the nervous system treated their patients with massages, mud packs, hot baths, rest cures, energy cures, electric sparks or whatever else seemed to relieve their mysterious ills. Sometimes their patients did improve, but nobody could be sure that it was because of the treatments. As one Viennese physician put it, "The patient recovered with, without or in spite of the doctor."

When Dr. Freud set up practice he outfitted his office with the best available equipment, but after twenty months he was forced to conclude that it did little for the neurotic patients he faced daily. He simply had to find better methods of treatment if he was to help.

Since his training in France had convinced him that the discomforts of most of those who came to see him were not caused by any organic damage, he decided to try his hand at hypnotism. Charcot had used it extensively at the Salpêtrière and Freud was also impressed by the work of

DR. SIGMUND FREUD, SPECIALIST IN NERVOUS DISORDERS

Liébeault and Bernheim, so much so that, in 1888, he translated, into German, Dr. Bernheim's book on hypnotic suggestion.

When Freud started to use hypnotism regularly in his practice, in 1887, the results were satisfying. For a while he thought he had found a cure for hysteria. But he soon discovered that the recovery of many patients was short-lived. And then there was another difficulty. Some of his patients could not be hypnotized; they would stay awake no matter how much he entreated them to go to sleep.

Freud decided that his technique might be at fault and that he needed more experience. So in the summer of 1889, he went to Nancy to visit Dr. Bernheim and perfect his skill as a hypnotist, taking along a patient in whom he had repeatedly failed to induce a deep state of hypnosis. During the following weeks, Freud watched Bernheim's procedure. When the patients were in a trance state they were told — often commanded — that they would feel healthy when they awoke. And their symptoms did disappear, at least for the time being. Bernheim, however, agreed with Freud that not all patients could be hypnotized, and he, too, failed to induce a deep trancelike state in Freud's patient.

Nevertheless, Freud was enthusiastic again and returned to Vienna to treat his patients the same way. Occasionally, he had remarkable results, but even those he was able to help soon had relapses, or substituted another symptom for the one that had "disappeared." Freud again questioned whether hypnotic suggestion could work permanent cures. Besides, it was frustrating to keep repeating to a patient that his symptoms were "imaginary." Although the symptoms did not have a well-defined physical cause, they were nevertheless real, and both he and the patient knew it. It seemed senseless to deny the existence of the illness and at the same time "talk it away" as if by magic.

In any case, Freud knew that he was not getting closer to uncovering the causes of neuroses, although, as he later wrote, he had the "profoundest impression of the possibilities that there could be powerful mental processes which . . . remained hidden from the consciousness of man."

At about this time he recalled his conversations with his old friend, Dr. Joseph Breuer, about the hysteria of Anna O. While the case had impressed him at the time — enough to discuss it with Charcot when he was in Paris — he had put it out of his mind when the French neurologist was unimpressed. Having reached a dead end in the treatment of his own neurotic patients, Freud went to see Breuer and made him recount the details of the case. In Breuer's opinion Anna's symptoms were a substitute for strong repressed feelings of resentment and guilt toward her sick father. Breuer had observed that during hypnosis she was able to recount, in great detail, the circumstances under which her neurotic symptoms first appeared, and somehow, gradually, this process had rid Anna of her physical symptoms.

Since this method seemed to be a step toward uncovering the origin of neuroses, Freud adopted it in treating his own patients. During the next few years, Freud and Breuer met frequently and, in 1895, they jointly published a book, *Studies in Hysteria,* that relates the case of Anna O. as well as four cases of hysteria treated by Freud.

In their introduction to this work, the physicians wrote

that suppressed painful emotions can produce hysterical illness directly or symbolically related to the original event. The memory of this original event, which has become unconscious, then acts as a "foreign body" that must be disposed off before the patient recovers his health. To their great surprise, the authors found "that each individual hysterical symptom immediately and permanently disappeared when we had succeeded in bringing clearly to light the memory of the event by which it was provoked and in arousing its accompanying affect [emotion]."

Freud and Breuer pointed out that language acknowledges man's need to "discharge" emotions which accompany everyday occurrences. One speaks of "crying oneself out" or "blowing off steam." Also, injuries suffered in silence — "mortifications" — are often considered the worst of all.

Relations between Breuer and Freud, warm and friendly for years, became so strained as the *Studies on Hysteria* neared completion that each author wrote a separate theoretical interpretation of their findings. For Breuer, the case of Anna O. remained only an interlude in a busy practice, and he looked upon Freud, for whom it was the beginning of his theory of psychoanalysis, "as a hen at a hawk."

One of the patients, whose case Freud reported in the *Studies,* was a young woman of twenty-four, Elisabeth von R. Aside from all the other difficulties involved in her treatment, she was one of those who could not be hypnotized. When Freud saw her she was hardly able to walk. After two years of consulting one physician after another, she was sent to Freud, who in those days saw many patients for whom nobody else could do anything.

Since she could not be hypnotized, Freud feared that he, too, would be unable to help her, or should he try, just try, to treat her while she was awake?

Freud instructed Elisabeth, who was relaxing on a couch, to concentrate on the symptoms of her illness and to report faithfully everything that came to her mind, even if it seemed unimportant, inappropriate, silly, embarrassing or unpleasant. To help her in this search for forgotten memories, Freud kept questioning her relentlessly.

But Elisabeth did not need any urging. She could "see things in front of her mind's eyes as if they were printed pages in a picture book." One day she reprimanded Freud for continually interrupting her with his prying questions.

Fortunately, Freud was an excellent listener. From then on, he let Elisabeth and his other patients follow their own train of thought. He learned that such seemingly blind meanderings would in the end arrive at the source of the patient's trouble. Freud called this process, in which one thought follows another, *free association*.

Through free association, Freud's patients started to reveal things he never would have suspected otherwise. Freud also discovered that his patients could be helped only if they cooperated. To obtain such cooperation he had to make them feel that he, the doctor, was worthy of their trust. It was a two-way process.

Freud realized that Elisabeth had trouble telling him certain things. Often, when she claimed that no thought would come to her mind, Freud knew, from the tense expression on her face, that it was not so. Deeper probing always revealed that she was struggling with something she wanted to hide from herself and from others. Freud was to call this reluctance to remember certain things *resistance*.

Months passed. Freud, who had spent so much time learning to listen to a person's chest with a stethoscope, instead listened patiently to the thoughts of Elisabeth von R. She was an invalid, who not so long ago had been the center of a happy family. Her father had died and Elisabeth looked after her lonely mother. She rejoiced when her favorite sister came to visit with her husband — a man so attractive that Elisabeth would have been happy to call him her own. Such feeling had to be *repressed*. But a little later the sister died, and when Elisabeth looked at her on her deathbed, the thought flashed through her mind that her brother-in-law was a free man, and in need of a new wife. This thought was immediately forgotten and buried, but Elisabeth's legs felt heavy and painful; she became an invalid, too sick to please any man, too preoccupied with herself to worry about "forbidden dreams."

In the long hours Freud and his patient spent together analyzing her thoughts, he discovered why Elisabeth might have "chosen" her legs to be the physical source of her discomfort. One day, shortly before her sister died, Elisabeth took a long hike with her brother-in-law. Once again she felt how much this man suited her. When she came home her body ached from tiredness and her soul from guilt.

Freud had difficulties in making Elisabeth face the fact that she was in love with her sister's husband. At first she wept, then she said that "it could not be true," that "she was incapable of such wickedness," that "she could never forgive herself for it." It took a lot of persuasion on Freud's part before she was at all impressed by his two pieces of consolation: "that we are not responsible for our feelings," and "that her behavior, the fact that she had fallen ill in these circumstances, was sufficient evidence of her moral character."

In the end, she accepted Freud's interpretation and recovered, and her case was additional proof to Freud that the mind is able to handle unacceptable wishes as long as they are faced squarely.

Freud was satisfied with the way in which he had treated Elisabeth von R. He called this method of treatment *psychoanalysis*. "Psyche" is the Greek word for soul, and Freud felt that his patient's trouble had disappeared through careful *analysis* or examination of her thoughts and feelings. From then on he made few changes in the method by which he treated his patients, though in time he became much more skilled in interpreting the "language of the mind."

Freud took great pleasure in Elisabeth's recovery. A few months after he ceased to treat her, he made a special effort to attend a dance at which he knew his former patient would be. From afar he happily watched her glide across the dance floor on the arm of a handsome young man.

Freud had few such professional pleasures in those days. He had cured Elisabeth von R. and made life tolerable for other neurotic patients, but he knew that he was far from understanding the workings of the mind. He was certain he had to go further, and to do so he had to plunge deeply into his own unconscious. But how was he, the first psychoanalyst, going to examine his own mind?

His patients often told him their dreams which, like all dreams, seemed a hopeless jumble of utter nonsense. But were they really nonsense? The ancients had tried to use dreams to forecast the future. Dr. Freud realized that there was no substance to this, but perhaps dreams could be used as clues to one's past, and he started to examine his own dreams and those of his friends, patients and children. He collected dreams as other people collect postage stamps. Soon he had collected more than a thousand dreams.

Some dreams — especially those of children — were easy to understand. His little daughter Anna, for instance, was dreaming of strawberries and other good things to eat the night after she had been denied food because of an upset stomach. Obviously Anna was fulfilling her wish for food. But for grownups things were more complicated.

At times, dream interpretation seemed a hopeless task. Freud was convinced more than ever that dreams do have a meaning and he was like an archaeologist trying to crack the code of a lost language. If he could learn to interpret dreams, the road to the unconscious part of the mind would be wide open. Then perhaps he would be able to "cure all the incurable nervous patients" who found their way into his examining room. But he was still far from having cracked the code. He was lonely and mystified and even gave up lecturing at the University because, as he wrote, he did not wish to talk about "things I do not understand."

While he was so engaged, his father lay dying. He was a very old man, but his death revived in Freud memories of earlier days, when there had been a fierce rivalry between father and son. Rivalry for what, the son now wondered. Was such a burning rivalry between father and son peculiar to the Freud family, or was this a more general phenomenon?

Freud listened to his patients with a deeper understanding. He also observed his young sons and daughters, and recalled that *he* had always been his mother's favorite. He, too, had loved his mother in a special way, and although in time Freud had grown to respect his father, he never felt the same devotion and affection for his father as he did toward his mother. Eventually, all these thoughts and observations took shape, and, together with his interpretation of dreams, became the cornerstone of his psychoanalytical teachings. Of both he was to say later, "It seems to be my fate to discover only the obvious: that children have sexual feelings, which every nursemaid knows; and that night dreams are just as much a wish fulfillment as day dreams."

Freud believed that children are born with sexual impulses which undergo a definite pattern of development until they emerge in the normal adult form. At first, a baby is only aware of his own body. For pleasure he rocks himself, sucks his thumb and anything else he can grasp. Since the infant's love is centered on himself, Freud called this the *narcissistic stage*, after the Greek youth Narcissus, who had been fated to fall in love with his own reflection.

Gradually an infant's world expands; he leaves his crib, toddles about and becomes aware of those around him; he can love others besides himself. At that time, Freud said, it is natural for children to draw closer to the parent of the opposite sex. Little boys want to monopolize their mother's love, sometimes to the point of openly resenting their father. Little girls, on the other hand, seek the love of their father. Freud called this period the *Oedipal stage*, after the legend of Oedipus, the mythological Greek king, who in ignorance and because it had been so destined, slew his father and married his mother. When this stage passes, like most early childhood memories, it is seemingly forgotten. Freud, however, believed that memories relating to it are not forgotten but repressed.

By the time children go to school they have reached the *latency period* — a period at which sexual feelings are dormant. Clubs and gangs are great favorites. Boys seem closest to boys, girls to girls. At home each child tries to follow the footsteps of the parent of its own sex. Girls like to imitate their mothers, and boys emulate the more masculine ways of their fathers. During adolescence, when the entire body prepares itself for adult life, sexual feelings gradually become more mature and directed.

Sometimes, however, just as physical development is off schedule or stunted, emotional development may also become warped. Instead of passing smoothly from one phase to the next, a child may become *fixated* in a particular state. These persons retain some of their infantile behavior patterns, clinging perhaps to such childish activities as thumb-sucking or bed-wetting. Other neurotic patients, in whom such behavior was suppressed, convert their infantile behavior into vomiting, headaches, stuttering, excessive eating and scores of other symptoms that profit so little from ordinary medical treatment.

In analysis, Freud's patients were able to relive some of the stages of their emotional development. They transferred to their analyst some of the feelings of resentment, hate, jealousy and guilt they had experienced for or toward their mothers and fathers, brothers or sisters. They were able to complete their emotional growth and dissolve the bonds that kept them fixated at a childish emotional level.

By 1897, Freud was no longer exclusively concerned with the well-being of others. He wrote to Dr. Wilhelm

Fliess, a Berlin nose and throat specialist with whom he corresponded extensively, "the chief patient I am busy with is myself." Freud was in the process of undergoing a self-analysis, and rigorously examined his own dreams, moods and fantasies as if they belonged to someone else.

This was no easy task, and Freud sometimes passed through a "curious state of mind which one's consciousness cannot apprehend: twilight thoughts, a veil over one's mind, scarcely a ray of light here and there." And then: "I believe I am in a cocoon, and God knows what kind of beast will creep out of it." Slowly, however, Freud felt that his own problems were yielding to self-analysis, and, by 1899, he reported that it had done him a great deal of good since he was much more normal than he was four or five years earlier.

His analysis revealed that he had many of the same Oedipal feelings and infantile sexual wishes he had observed in his patients, and he felt certain enough of his findings to conclude that they are a "general phenomenon of early childhood."

Dreams continued to haunt Freud, and he was convinced that all dreams — even those that are terrible and frightening — fulfill a wish. His patients rebelled at this idea. They dreamt of the death of beloved relatives, they dreamt they walked naked in a public place, they dreamt that they were giving a big party, on a Sunday, when all the stores were closed and they could not buy food. "How could they wish these things to happen?" they asked. "Yes," Professor Freud might say, "you did wish your brother dead, perhaps not now, but when you both were small and you each wanted all your parents' love. Perhaps you dreamt that you were scantily dressed in a public place because you wanted to attract attention. And as far as that party is concerned, you might really not have wanted to give it. Who were some of the people you had invited?"

Delving into his own unconscious, Freud discovered that much of what his patients told him of their early childhood had not taken place. The unconscious often cannot distinguish between what has really happened and what has only happened in *fantasy*.

There was so much to explore and to learn. He reached the conclusion that Elisabeth's troubles had not started the day she stood at her sister's deathbed but were rooted in childhood, when she also had failed to face up to feelings she could not accept. Because they were unacceptable, she *repressed* them into her unconscious, as one would hide a piece of dirty linen from public view. Freud's patients recovered, once they accepted the things they were ashamed of, as well as the fact that they were less noble, less loving, less brave than they wished or thought they ought to be.

It might seem a simple matter "to accept oneself," but the mind takes great pains to hide its "dirty linen." Special training is needed to pick out, from the flood of words spoken by a patient in analysis, those facts which can be used as a key to his unconscious. Over the years, Freud developed a symbolic language which helped him to understand his patients better.

Freud discovered that dreams were not the only channel through which the unconscious speaks. Forgotten words and slips of the tongue are another method of communication. For instance, everyone assumes that vacations are more fun than the school year. And yet, if someone remarks, "I wish that June would come *later* than sooner" (instead of saying, "I wish that June would come sooner than later"), he may, at the bottom of his heart, prefer the school year to vacation time. Again, if someone dials Joe's telephone number, instead of dialing John's — as he had intended to do — he may have, unconsciously, wanted to speak to the person whose number he had dialed by mistake. Today such mistakes are called "Freudian slips," because Freud had discovered that such slips often have a meaning.

For years Freud had been working on *The Interpretation of Dreams*, the book which explains his dream theory. He felt, once the book was published, the medical profession could not fail to take notice of him. In one of his daydreams, Freud had wondered whether someday a memorial plaque would adorn the summer house in which he had worked on the manuscript:

IN THIS HOUSE ON JULY 24, 1895
THE SECRET OF DREAMS WAS REVEALED TO
DR. SIGMUND FREUD

In 1900 — the dawn of a new century — *The Interpretation of Dreams* was finally published. It was not the success Freud hoped it would be. Like its author, it was to be ignored for many years.

Freud, however, knew it to be a great book — and that it would remain his greatest no matter how many other books he would write. As he said later, "Insight such as this falls to one's lot but once in a lifetime."

10 PSYCHOANALYSIS LEAVES VIENNA

Freud's entire life was centered on his Vienna home at Berggasse 19. Downstairs he saw his patients; upstairs he was pampered by Martha, who had become a devoted wife and loving mother. Together they watched their six children, Mathilde, Sophie, Martin, Oliver, Ernst and Anna, grow to adulthood. Mathilde, the eldest, was named for Joseph Breuer's wife; Martin bore the name of Jean-Martin Charcot; Oliver that of Oliver Cromwell, Freud's early hero; and Ernst was named for Ernst Bruecke, the professor of physiology for whom Freud had worked in his early years. Except at mealtime, to which it was unthinkable to be late, the children saw little of their father during most of the year. But in the summer, the whole family spent a couple of months together in the mountains, where they hiked, picked mushrooms and wild strawberries, read, wrote, swam and wandered about the woods.

Professionally, Freud felt like Robinson Crusoe on an island all by himself. He had no friends; even Breuer — who had lent him money while he was struggling, and with whom he had written his first book telling the story of Anna O. and Elisabeth von R. — now ignored him. During these lonely years, Freud's only audience was his friend, Dr. Wilhelm Fliess, and his sister-in-law, Minna Bernays, who had joined the Freud household in 1896.

In 1902, Freud felt a great need to share his knowledge with others. He announced that he was going to lecture once a week on the new theory of psychoanalysis.

When he arrived at the amphitheater of the Vienna General Hospital on the appointed evening, he found that he had only three listeners. But as the winter progressed, his audience grew to about twelve. Some of his listeners, who included doctors and medical students, were so impressed that they prevailed upon Freud to give them psychoanalytic treatment and training at regular meetings in his home. It was evident to Freud, from the beginning, that no one should practice psychoanalysis unless he had gained some insight into his own unconscious. Today, a full personal psychoanalysis is one of the requirements every future psychoanalyst has to meet.

Little by little, Freud's circle grew, and his reputation spread. He was no longer a psychoanalyst in complete isolation; others had read and heard of him, and soon a small number of psychoanalysts met, every Wednesday night, in Freud's home for study and discussion. Almost as soon as his ideas became known and gained adherents, they also came under severe attack from critics within and outside the medical profession, and Freud was a frequent target of the local newspapers.

In 1904, he received a letter from Dr. Eugen Bleuler,

one of the foremost psychiatrists of the century, telling him that he, his assistant, Carl G. Jung, and his staff had been most impressed by *The Interpretation of Dreams,* and that they were using dream interpretation and Freud's other concepts in various ways in the Burghoelzli Mental Hospital in Zurich. Recognition had come at last, for, at the beginning of the twentieth century, the Burghoelzli in Switzerland had taken the place of the Salpêtrière as the foremost mental institution in Europe.

In 1908, Freud, Bleuler, Jung and forty others assembled to discuss "Freudian psychology" in the small Austrian town of Salzburg — renowned as the birthplace of Mozart.

That same year Freud received an invitation to lecture at Clark University in Worcester, Massachusetts, and, on August 21, 1909, he set sail for the New World, aboard the German ship, S.S. *George Washington.* When he discovered that the cabin steward was reading his *Psychopathology of Everyday Life,* he smiled. The medical world might be slow to accept psychoanalysis, but his ideas had evidently left the doctors' offices and were being discussed in the world at large.

Freud was then fifty-three. His hair, his mustache and beard were greying. His opinion was now valued not only by neurologists, but by philosophers, writers and painters. The famous and the humble sought his advice. He was generous with his correspondence, and promptly answered every letter he received, no matter from whom. In his life he wrote many thousands of letters, all in longhand.

But the peaceful life of an elder statesman was not to be Freud's lot. Soon quarrels, caused partially by his domineering personality, broke out within the newly founded International Association. Some of Freud's oldest collaborators left, and in 1914, Carl G. Jung, the Swiss psychiatrist of whose support Freud was so proud, resigned as president of the society. Jung was to develop a psychoanalytic doctrine of his own.

In 1914, World War I broke out, and darkness descended over Europe. Freud's sons and sons-in-law were drafted; his pupils returned to their homelands, and the fledgling psychoanalytical association went into hibernation. Freud was once more isolated. He saw his patients as usual, however, and continued to investigate the soul of man.

His opinion of man had never been high. He was convinced that each man struggles with savage feelings, painfully subdued by thousands of years of civilized living. Accordingly, a man's first impulse is to hit when offended, to kill when angry, to run when in danger, to take what he wants. But civilization could not exist if everyone acted in this fashion. Running is no longer the best way to survive; hostile impulses have to be subdued, and reason dominates our material transactions. A newborn baby screams when it is hungry; it is taught to wait for its meals, not to hit when it is angry, to leave what is not his, and perhaps, to say "no, thank you," when offered a tempting piece of candy. And yet, in spite of this careful training, Freud believed, there remains within each person a savage, untamed instinct necessary for survival.

Freud called the conflicting parts of man's personality the *ego* — or I — and the *id*. The ego represents reason and sanity, in contrast to the id — the part of the mind where primitive and blind feelings live. As a child grows up, it develops a sort of internal censor that Freud called the *superego* or *ego ideal* — commonly called conscience.

Within all human beings Freud saw conflicts between

Sigmund Freud, 1920.

the ego, the id and the superego; between unbridled instincts and the limits imposed by society. Sometimes, the internal censor might set its standards too high and the individual feels unduly guilty. Sometimes, the id is too strong, or the ego too weak, and a person feels frustrated, or afraid.

Freud discovered that some of the nervous disorders of his patients were caused by such internal conflicts. This strife can manifest itself in many forms: feelings of anxiety, anguish, guilt, helplessness, despair, physical illness, inability to work or to get along with others. The aim of psychoanalytic treatment is, so to speak, to put a person's mental house in order. Elisabeth von R. recovered when she made peace with the fact that she wanted her sister's husband — and yet she knew that it was inappropriate for her even to wish for such an alliance.

In 1918, when the war came to an end, international psychoanalytic friendships were renewed. Many Americans came to Vienna to study psychoanalysis with Dr. Freud.

In 1930, Freud was awarded the Goethe prize for literature. Goethe — one of the great German writers — had always been beloved by Freud. Perhaps he felt close to Geothe's hero Faust who, when he sold his soul to the devil, did not ask for fame or riches but rather for supernatural knowledge.

Freud was too ill to travel to Frankfurt to accept the prize in person, and his daughter Anna accepted the citation in his behalf. Anna was the only one of Freud's children to follow in his footsteps. In her most important work, *The Ego and the Mechanisms of Defense,* published in 1936, she modified and expanded her father's concept of the ego's role in reconciling impulses received from the id with demands made by the superego. Anna Freud also played an important part in the development of child psychology, and founded, and still heads, the Hampstead Child Therapy Clinic in London.

Even as a child, Freud had collected mementoes of past civilizations. Glassed-in cabinets, filled with Greek, Egyptian and Etruscan statuettes, lined the walls of his study. This collection and trips to places, where Western civilization was born, were the only luxuries in which he had indulged himself. Wasn't his life's work devoted to understanding man's mind? And wasn't such an understanding rooted in man's past?

Freud had gone to Rome for the first time in 1902. Almost immediately he had visited the statue of Moses, carved out of marble by Michelangelo 400 years earlier. Freud felt a special kinship for the leader who had taken the Jewish people out of Egyptian bondage and taught them to believe in a single God. When Freud gazed at Moses' marble image he was struck by his expression, "a mixture of wrath, pain and contempt."

Seven times Freud returned to Rome; each time he would stare at Michelangelo's Moses. In his right hand the prophet was clutching the marble tablets on which the Ten Commandments were engraved. Moses was looking at the Jews who, during his trip up Mount Sinai, had fallen back to worshiping a golden calf. Moses' face expresses wrath and fury, but his gestures betray the fact that he had mastered his impulse to smash the tablets onto the ground. He would continue to be the leader of his erring people, and the prophet who would lead them to the Promised Land.

"The Sleep of Reason Produces Monsters" by Francisco Goya (Spanish, 1746-1828). Goya, asleep, is haunted by a nightmare. One of the owls is handing him a brush—urging him to paint. Goya is reputed to have said about this etching: "Imagination deserted by reason begets impossible monsters. United with reason, she is the mother of all art, and the source of its wonders."

In 1933 his people — the Jews — were again in great need of a leader to take them out of bondage. Hitler had come to power in Germany, and among those slated for extermination were the Jews, the gypsies and the mentally ill.

Freud had grown old and renowned. On his eightieth birthday, Vienna had finally awakened to the fact that it had a famous son. On this occasion, the mail for Berggasse 19 was so heavy that the city had to set up a special post office, and the Austrian Minister of Education came in person to present his good wishes.

Then, as now, his ideas were hotly debated by the medical world. Rarely before had one doctor's findings generated such vehement opposition as well as fierce loyalty. Even today, there are several rival "schools" of psychoanalysis that continue the quarrels which arose so early in its history. Regardless of their theoretical leanings, however, all these groups use, to a large extent, the techniques that Freud developed for the treatment of his patients in Vienna.

But Freud's influence is not limited to psychiatry. It is felt in art, drama, literature, philosophy, the rearing of children, the way people look at themselves. And when such words are used as "complex," "block," "conflict," "aggression," "ego," "sense of guilt," "father figure," little thought is given to the man who first formulated these ideas.

The belated recognition at home did Freud little good. He was ill. Since 1923, he had been suffering from cancer of the jaw. Countless operations kept the enemy at bay, but, in 1938, the end was near. Neither fame nor illness would protect him from the Nazi invaders, who marched into

Austria that year, and Freud's friends urged him to leave Vienna. But how could he abandon his four elderly sisters? How could he leave the house in which he had lived for forty-seven years? The Nazis stormed his home, took away his passport, as well as his money and books, and Freud became a prisoner in Vienna.

His friends persisted. The President of the United States, Franklin Delano Roosevelt, wired to Vienna on Freud's behalf, and Princess Marie Bonaparte — the sister of the King of Greece and a longtime friend and pupil of Freud's — came in person. She paid the Nazis a ransom of a quarter of a million Austrian schillings, and on June 4, 1938, Freud and his family left for England, "the island in a silver sea" that for Freud had always meant freedom. England gave Freud a hero's welcome. His house, overlooking Regent's Park in London, was bursting with flowers, and a few valuable antiques were sent by people who thought that Freud's own would be lost for good. Taxi drivers knew where he lived and, within a few days, mail addressed to "Dr. Freud, London," was delivered without delay.

Three months later Freud's furniture and his cherished collection of antiques arrived in England, and loving hands transformed his room in a foreign land into a study that closely resembled the one he had occupied so long in Vienna.

But Freud's health was deteriorating rapidly. The cancer that was destroying his jaw inched toward the throat. He could not eat, or smoke, or talk properly, but he continued to write, even though his pen was "no longer the same."

And in London — far from Vienna where all his life he had suffered from being a Jew — he was finishing his last book: *Moses and Monotheism,* a psychoanalytic study of

Sigmund Freud's consulting room in London. Note collection of antiques and, on the wall, picture of Jean-Martin Charcot with hysterical patient.

religion. Examining all available evidence — Moses' name, the Bible, the myths surrounding the origins of other folk heroes or leaders, and the religious history of Egypt at the time of the Exodus — Freud concluded that Moses, the lawgiver of the Jews, was not a Jew, but an Egyptian.

Freud died on the 23rd of September, 1939, at the age of eighty-three. His ashes were placed in the Grecian urn of which he had said, when he received it from Princess

Marie Bonaparte on his seventy-fifth birthday, "It is a pity one cannot take it into one's grave."

Freud had ushered in a new age in psychiatry. His convictions echoed what Philippe Pinel had said years earlier. "How dare we fix the limits which divide what is normal from what borders on a state of illness?"

11 SHOCKED TO THEIR SENSES

> Manfred Sakel: 1900-1957
> Ugo Cerletti: 1877-1963

Men ought to know that from the brain and from the brain only arise our pleasures, joys, laughter, and jests as well as our sorrows, pains, griefs and tears . . . It is the same thing which makes us mad or delirious, inspires us with dread and fear, whether by night or by day, brings sleeplessness, inopportune mistakes, aimless anxieties, absent-mindedness and acts that are contrary to habit. . . .

Hippocrates (460-377 B.C.)

Since early times, physicians have vacillated between an organic and a psychological approach to mental illness. In the nineteenth and twentieth century, when so much progress was made in all of medicine, both sides advanced steadily. Though Charcot, Freud and others had clearly shown that functional neurosis and hysteria are caused by emotional factors, it seemed only a matter of time until other types of mental illness could be attributed to organic causes.

This was not a modern concept. Hippocrates, the "father of medicine," recognized no separation between the body and the soul, between physical suffering and mental anguish. He did not know their cause, but he looked upon illnesses as a natural phenomenon, and not a punishment meted out by angry gods.

He had few weapons with which to combat disease, and firmly believed in "waiting on the natural healing power of the body." He was also a keen observer, describing and classifying many diseases, including mental ailments. Among these he distinguished epilepsy, mania, paranoia and hysteria. The last, he thought, was caused by a "wandering uterus." Twenty-two centuries later, Jean-Martin Charcot in Paris demonstrated that men, too, can suffer from hysteria, and that regardless of what it is due to, hysteria cannot be caused by a "wandering uterus."

Hippocrates was the first among those who believed that mental illness, like other diseases, stems from physical causes. These champions of the mentally ill were not without evidence to support their beliefs. Was it not likely that persons whose mind became deranged after a violent accident had suffered some brain damage? And what about the many "sane and respected" adults who grew childish, confused, forgetful or even downright "mad" with old age? They, too, seemed to suffer from verifiable organic changes.

One argument, advanced by those who, like Benjamin Rush, believed that insanity is caused by definite organic changes of the body, was that high fevers and certain common infections — such as measles, influenza, and scarlet fever — would, on occasion, impair the brain and mental functioning.

Curiously, the reverse was also true, and had already been observed by Hippocrates. In a few instances, an attack of malarial fever had brought some insane back to sanity. Once, during the Middle Ages, a severe cholera epidemic had swept through a French asylum, leaving hundreds of dead in its wake. But, among the survivors were a few who had recovered their mental facilities in the course of the illness.

In despair, people had also tried to shock the insane back to their senses. In Switzerland in times long past, it was customary to put lunatics into nets, lower them into a freezing lake and pull them up just before they drowned. The theory behind the treatment was to make it unpleasant

"Whirling Cage"—an old-time device for calming mental patients, by John De Pol.

for the demon which had taken possession of the soul. Though this procedure was not a surefire cure, it seemed to have worked on occasion.

But the man who developed "shock therapy" into a modern method of treatment for the mentally ill stumbled upon it by accident — or despair — for like his colleagues, he was overwhelmed by the suffering of his patients and his inability to alleviate their plight.

Manfred Sakel was born in Austria in 1900. He was a Jew who traced back his ancestry some 800 years to Maimonides, the great physician and philosopher born in twelfth-century Spain. Maimonides' true love was the Torah (The Five Books of Moses).

He started to practice medicine out of economic necessity, and quickly became one of the most beloved and sought-after physicians of his times, attending, as he wrote to a friend:

> Jews and Gentiles, nobles and common people, judges and bailiffs, friends and foes — a mixed multitude.

He felt that:

> Besides the power to heal, a doctor must possess an independent mind . . . he must be a whole man, observant, cautious, and attentive to each patient on the presumption that his case is individual and special.

It was perhaps the spirit of these words that inspired his descendant-across-the-centuries to devote himself to psychiatry, a branch of medicine in great need of doctors with independent, observant minds.

After graduating from the University of Vienna Medical School in 1925, Manfred Sakel was appointed to the Lichterfelde Hospital in Berlin — a small institution. Among its patients there were some who were trying to rid themselves of addiction to morphine.

Sakel understood that his patients had taken to drugs to escape the reality of a world they could not bear. He believed, however, that in cases of prolonged addiction, drugs radically changed the chemistry of the body, chiefly of the nervous system, and that only some counterphysical measure would restore it to normalcy. Perhaps, Sakel thought, the change in the body chemistry was related in some way to hormones, which, at the time, were making front-page medical news.

The hormone, insulin, had recently been discovered and isolated by Frederick Banting and Charles H. Best, in Canada. Insulin regulates sugar utilization in the body. In healthy people, the hormone is manufactured by special cells embedded in the pancreas. Diabetics lack insulin, and do not process sugar properly. This defect is so serious that untreated diabetics almost invariably died within a few years after the disease declared itself. In 1922, the two Canadian scientists discovered that such patients could be saved with regular supplies of insulin, obtained from the pancreas of calves.

In his search for "a counterphysical measure," Sakel's thoughts turned to insulin — this newly discovered chemical that wrought wonders. Perhaps, by chance, it would do something for his miserable patients who were so valiantly trying to regain freedom from drugs.

A few animal experiments, crudely carried out in his kitchen, gave Sakel the courage to try. He needed a great deal of courage, for he knew that if he lost a single patient through "experimentation," it meant the end of his medical career. But his patients did not die. As the insulin slowly entered their agitated bodies, they relaxed and were soon asleep — the first healthful sleep they had had in weeks. After a few hours many woke up refreshed, clear of mind and willing to face the trials and tribulations of everyday life.

Morphine addicts, however, occupied only a part of Sakel's time; he was also in charge of schizophrenics. *Schizophrenia* literally means "split mind." It is not only the most common mental illness — at least half of all hospitalized mentally ill in the United States suffer from it — but also the least understood. The symptoms of schizophrenia are varied. Some patients completely withdraw from the world; others are violent and aggressive. There are those who refuse to talk, and those whose speech becomes so garbled that it resembles a "word salad." As far as anyone knew in the 1920's, the disease was completely hopeless and incurable.

It was this very hopelessness that persuaded Manfred Sakel to try insulin treatment on gravely ill schizophrenics. He planned to administer the hormone until his patients fell into a deep slumber.

However, treatment with insulin is tricky; it was even more so in the early days when the hormone was first discovered. An excess of the drug causes *insulin shock*: loss of consciousness, violent convulsions and perhaps even death. Fortunately, insulin shock can easily be reversed by administration of a quickly assimilated sugar — *glucose*. When Sakel treated his patients, he always kept a syringe full of glucose solution within easy reach for those who, in spite of his caution, had entered a state of shock.

As time progressed, and Sakel gained more confidence in using his novel method of treatment, he noted to his surprise that only those patients who had undergone shock had profited from his insulin therapy. Now he set out to induce shock deliberately, and, for the first time in medical history, a great many agitated psychotic patients seemed to have permanently recovered their sanity.

While Sakel was rediscovering the age-old theory of shock therapy and developing it into a scientific method of treatment, Hitler took over power in Germany, and so, in 1933, Sakel was obliged to leave Berlin. He returned to the Universitaetsklinik in Vienna, headed by Julius von Wagner-Jauregg, who himself had successfully treated some mentally ill by infecting them with malarial fever organisms. (For this discovery he had received the Nobel Prize in 1927, the only psychiatrist so honored.)

Sakel's stay in his native land was short, and, in 1936, he arrived in the United States. His method of treatment was readily accepted by clinicians throughout the United States, and he was soon to head the first conference on insulin therapy in psychiatry, held in America.

Until his death, in 1957, Manfred Sakel practiced psychiatry in New York City. Though in medical history he is remembered for developing insulin shock therapy, he himself recognized it to be only one of many forms of psychiatric treatment.

As news of successes obtained by physical treatment of mental illness spread throughout the medical world, more and more physicians became interested. One of these was an Italian, Ugo Cerletti. He was born in 1877 in the village of Conegliano, eighty miles north of Venice. He studied medicine in Rome and Turin, and, in order to specialize in neurology, completed his training in Germany and at the Salpêtrière in Paris, where he worked with Charcot's great successor, Professor Pierre Marie.

During the first thirty years of his professional life, Cerletti investigated the changes that take place in the nervous system during aging and disease, working in the field that had been pioneered by Charcot. Gradually, however, Cerletti's interest changed, and, when news of drug-induced shock treatments first appeared in the medical literature, he wondered whether shock could not be induced more easily and more safely with electricity.

By a quirk of fate he was not the first Italian to recommend electric treatment for "diseases of the head." In 47 A.D., Scribonius Largus, physician to Claudius, the Roman Emperor, had prescribed that:

> A chronic and intolerable headache which insistently manifests itself can be eliminated at once if treated by applying a live torpedo fish [electric eel], black in color, to the site of the pain and leaving it there until the pain stops and the part is swollen.

Since the Roman physician's day, man had tamed electricity and Cerletti did not have to rely on eels to supply the current. All he had to do was to attach electrodes to his patient's head and plug the equipment into the laboratory outlet. Unlike his predecessor, however, he ran the greater danger of electrocuting his patients.

Cerletti knew that the Italian slaughterhouses used electricity to stun pigs before slaughter. A few simple experiments would determine the amount of current that would make the difference between "reversible shock" and death. It soon became apparent that there was a sufficiently wide margin between a fatal quantity of electricity and one from which a pig or a dog would recover with little ill effect. Autopsy of electroshocked animals revealed that this procedure caused very minor changes in the structure of the brain.

When Cerletti was reasonably sure that electroshock did not cause permanent brain damage, he set out to find his first patient. As he said, "The case had to be a desperate one, for it is a tradition in medicine that novel treatments can only be used on hopeless cases for whom no safer therapy is available." He did not have to wait long. A severe schizophrenic from the northern part of Italy was admitted to his hospital in Rome. As one of Cerletti's co-workers recalled: "The man spoke an incomprehensible gibberish and was unable to say anything about himself — not even his name. When the electrodes were fastened to him, he certainly could not protest; he surely could not comprehend that he was destined to make medical history."

When everything was in order, Cerletti applied a weak electric shock, lasting only a tenth of a second. To everybody's surprise, the man sat up straight and burst into a loud song. Cerletti decided to follow the first treatment immediately by a second, lasting only two-tenths of a second. Before that could be done, however, the patient again sat up and said, in clear Italian, *"Non una seconda! Mortifera."* (Not again! It will kill me.)

In spite of the patient's plea, Cerletti persisted. The man received eleven more treatments; then he was discharged and went home, in full possession of his senses — at least for the time being.

Unfortunately, it turned out that although drug and electroshock therapy have held their place in the treatment of the mentally ill ever since their discovery — and are still used in the case of severely depressed patients — rarely do they produce lifetime cures. Their mode of action is also still a mystery. And so the search for the key to mental illness and for other remedies was continued on an ever-widening front.

12 THE MISSING LINK

Ivar Asbjørn Følling: 1888-

Because of a nail the shoe was lost
Because of the shoe the horse was lost
Because of the horse the rider was lost
Because of the rider the battle was lost
Because of the battle the war was lost
Because of the war the kingdom was lost
All on account of a horseshoe nail!

About forty years ago a young Norwegian mother, who chose to be remembered simply as Mrs. E., noticed that her baby was obviously "slower" than other children her age. The infant did not recognize familiar faces, roll around in her crib or play as did the children of Mrs. E.'s friends. As time passed, the difference in development became more pronounced. At two, the little girl barely walked, and later, never learned to say more than a few words. Her mother did her best to keep the child neat and clean, but in spite of frequent scrubbings, the little girl still had an unpleasant, dank smell about her, a smell one could scarcely forget after being exposed to it.

There was little doubt that the child was mentally retarded. Whatever the reason, her mind would never develop to its fullest potential; she would remain dependent on her family or become a lifelong resident in a home for the mentally retarded.

When the little girl was three years old, another child, a boy, was born into the family. Mrs. E. hopefully looked at his eager, bright features and wished that he would bring only joy. But after a few months the baby's eyes lost their luster, he stopped playing with his rattle and seemed to forget about the world surrounding his crib. And, strangely, he developed the same unpleasant smell that his sister had.

Mrs. E. started to take her children from doctor to doctor and from hospital to hospital. Perhaps nothing could be done to alleviate her plight, but she had to find out what was ailing her little family. Her efforts, however, were in vain; no satisfactory explanation was forthcoming.

Dr. E., a busy dentist, was even more affected than his wife. When at home, he could not stand to be in the same room with the children because he thought their peculiar smell aggravated his asthma!

One day he spoke about this to a colleague, who promptly suggested that the children be taken to Dr. Asbjørn Følling, a young Norwegian scientist trained both as a biochemist and as a medical doctor. Determined, Mrs. E. eagerly explored every new avenue, and, in 1934, when her children were four and seven years old, she took them to Følling.

Dr. Følling agreed that the peculiar smell of the siblings

Ivar Asbjørn Følling

warranted investigation. It pointed to a physical origin of the disease, and he started out with the analysis of their urine.

Uroscopy — or looking at a patient's urine — is medicine's oldest diagnostic test. It was practiced long before urine could be analyzed chemically, and for centuries the urine glass was as much the trademark of the physician as the stethoscope is today. Urine is a tangible indicator of the hidden labors of the body, and the presence, or absence, of certain specific chemical substances is one reflection of the state of health of the patient.

For instance, the urinary excretion of sugar is a clear-cut sign of diabetes, and as far back as the seventeenth century, the English physician Thomas Willis advised his students as follows: "Taste thy patient's urine. If it be sweet like honey he will waste away, grow weak, fall into sleep and die."

Though this particular urine test is very old — it was known to the ancient Egyptians — most of the tests currently used were developed during the last fifty years. When Mrs. E. went to consult Følling, he was engaged in studying acidosis, a symptom of several diseases, including diabetes, characterized by an abnormal composition of urine.

Følling first ascertained whether the children suffered from a chronic infection. When this possibility was ruled out, he tested for diacetic acid — a compound that sometimes appears in the urine of diabetics. He added the chemical, ferric chloride, and watched for the reddish-brown color that would develop if diacetic acid was present. To his surprise, however, the urine turned olive-green.

No such color appeared when he tested his own urine or that of other volunteers. Perhaps, he thought, the green color did not mean anything; it might have been caused by something the children had eaten, or by some special medicine their mother had given them. But the test came out the same when it was repeated on a fresh specimen of the children's urine.

Now Følling's curiosity was aroused to the fullest, and he asked whether Mrs. E. could collect twenty quarts of urine for him to work with. She certainly could and soon the doctor had the desired quantity with which to experiment. Now he worked feverishly extracting "it." As he recalled later, "I always knew where 'it' was because 'it' would give a green color with ferric chloride."

Within a week he had extracted "it"; after another month of hard work, "it" was a pure shiny, crystalline powder, looking very much like ordinary salt; in another six weeks, "it" proved to be *phenylpyruvic* acid.

Følling now collected urine samples from patients in Norwegian homes for the mentally ill and from a school for the mentally retarded. Among hundreds of urine samples tested, ten proved to contain phenylpyruvic acid. These belonged to severely retarded patients whose other symptoms also showed that they all suffered from the same illness.

Følling had discovered a new disease. He called it *phenylpyruvic oligophrenia* or "little brains caused by phenylpyruvic acid." For awhile it was also called "Følling's disease," but today it is mostly referred to as *phenylketonuria*, or PKU for short. It is a rare disease, affecting one out of every hundred institutionalized mentally retarded.

Naming the disease was the least of Dr. Følling's concerns. He wanted to know where phenylpyruvic acid came from. Unless he solved that puzzle he certainly could not hope to cure his patients.

To a biochemist, phenylpyruvic acid immediately suggests the amino acid, phenylalanine — one of the building blocks of proteins. Proteins, man's most important foodstuff, are complex molecules knitted together from twenty different amino acids, of which phenylalanine is one. Dr. Following's next plan was to investigate the fate of protein in the body or, to be more precise, the fate of phenylalanine because, once eaten, proteins are immediately broken down into their component amino acids.

In order to follow the path of Følling and other scientists, who by now had joined in the search, we must take a glimpse at what happens to food once it has been consumed.

The body operates like a very complex factory. It takes in food which is used for different purposes. Some of it is oxidized to release energy; some is used as raw material for building body tissue. The biochemist calls the sum total of tissue-building and energy-release processes *metabolism*.

Metabolism, which goes on in the cells after digested food is absorbed, involves thousands of small, interlocking chemical reactions following each other, step by step. The product formed in one reaction is not stored, but immediately becomes the starting material for the next reaction. In such an arrangement, the entire system relies on the proper functioning of every one of its component steps, no matter how trivial each step may seem.

An assembly line is manned by operators who have to do certain things, at certain times, to keep production flowing smoothly. If one of these operators decides to take off, his job remains undone and the next man down the line gets an imperfect product, which he cannot process properly. Soon the entire production line is glutted with defective, half-finished merchandise.

THE MISSING LINK

In living systems, the "operators" are *enzymes* — very special protein molecules tooled to do a specific job to a substance traveling down the metabolic pathway. Of course, enzymes and other key chemicals are manufactured by the body itself, and this is where this self-run factory differs from its man-made counterpart. Our metabolism "employs" hundreds of different enzymes. Considering the efficiency with which man operates twenty-four hours a day, seven days a week, for an average of seventy years, one can marvel at how well we are put together.

It so happens, however, that there are a few rare diseases in which one or the other of these key substances is either completely missing or present in insufficient amounts. In such a case there is "an error in the metabolism."

PKU results from such a metabolic error. It manifests itself within days after birth. The infant lacks the enzyme *phenylalanine hydroxylase,* normally made in the liver, which converts phenylalanine to the next member of the metabolic chain. Consequently, phenylalanine accumulates in the blood; some is transformed into abnormal products, among them phenylpyruvic acid, which Følling found in the urine of his patients.

The scientists then reasoned that if the severe retardation of children suffering from the disease was caused by the accumulation of phenylpyruvic acid and other abnormal breakdown products of phenylalanine, the affected children might develop normally if these substances could be prevented from accumulating. Perhaps all one needed to do was to put the affected babies on diets nearly free of phenylalanine.

This was easier said than done. The trouble was that phenylalanine is present in nearly all protein foods. Phenylalanine is part of the proteins in eggs, milk, meat and cheese. It would be possible to devise a nearly protein-free diet. Fruit, candy, green vegetables, rice, potatoes, oil and many other foods are more or less protein-free. But neither humans nor animals can survive on a protein-free diet. However, a protein food containing all the necessary amino acids, except phenylalanine, might do the trick.

It was relatively easy to break apart the protein molecules into their component amino acids, but sifting out phenylalanine from this "soup" of millions of small molecules was much more difficult. It was like sorting the entire mail of the United States and throwing away all the letters in sky-blue envelopes. Nevertheless, the scientists solved the problem, and soon they had a synthetic diet or baby formula — a phenylalanine-free protein food. When it was ready, they eagerly waited for a chance to use it, even though they would not know the final answer to their questions for years to come.

Would infants, doomed to a hopeless life in a mental institution, develop normally simply because they were receiving a special diet, one from which one-twentieth of the protein had been removed?

From the beginning, it was clear that PKU was a genetic disorder. The disease is extremely rare in the population at large, but occurs frequently in families affected by it. Therefore, each new birth in such a family is carefully watched and, in September, 1962, the attention of the public health authorities in Elkhart, Indiana, was focused on the forthcoming birth of Mr. and Mrs. Prentice's third child.

Visiting public health nurses had become acquainted with the Prentices some months previously, when the mother had requested that their fifteen-year-old daughter Marie be placed in a state institution for the mentally retarded.

Marie was a total invalid, who had never walked, talked or dressed herself. Those around her knew that she could hear, but nobody was quite sure that she could see. Since birth, her parents had cared for her with love and devotion, but, being pregnant, Mrs. Prentice could no longer lift the eighty-two-pound child. Concern for Marie was only one of Mrs. Prentice's burdens; she feared that the baby she was carrying would also be "invisibly marked" and as retarded as her oldest daughter.

After examining Marie, the nurse decided to test her for phenylpyruvic acid. The nurse's hunch proved correct. Marie was positive. This diagnosis gave substance to Mrs. Prentice's fears. Though the family had a completely normal son, there was one chance in four that the new baby would suffer from PKU.

Thirteen days after Bonnie Prentice was born, chemical blood and urine analysis indicated that she did have phenylketonuria. But her parents could take heart. The tedious sorting of the amino acid soup had paid off handsomely. As the scientists had hoped, it had been established that PKU-positive children are born with a completely normal intelligence which continues to develop normally if they are raised on a diet containing very little phenylalanine. To be effective, this diet has to be given within months after birth, otherwise the brain is damaged irreversibly.

By 1962, when Bonnie was born, Lofenalac — a food low in phenylalanine — was made commercially by one of the large drug companies. It is available to all who need it.

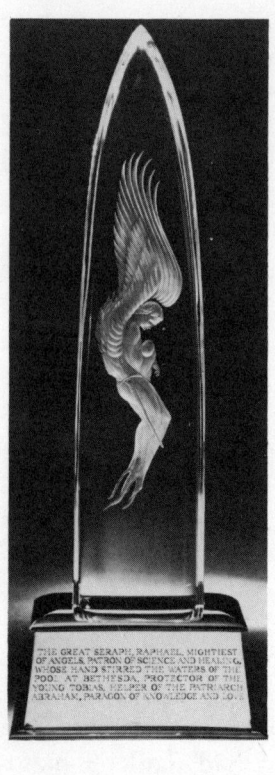

The figure on the Steuben crystal trophy represents Raphael, angel of science, healing and love, who brings hope to those whose lives are burdened with illness and infirmity.

For his work on phenylketonuria, Dr. Følling received an award from the Joseph P. Kennedy Jr. Foundation.

Raising Bonnie, however, will not be an easy matter. Long before she will understand why, she will be taught to bypass hamburgers, frankfurters, ice cream and other party foods. She will have countless blood tests to make sure that she has enough, but not too much phenylalanine, for, as it turned out, even *she* needs some of this important amino acid. But so far the child is healthy, of normal intelligence and a great source of pride and joy to everyone who helped her be that way; her parents, the nurse who spotted the disease in her older sister and all those who took part in the conquest of PKU — one of the first preventable forms of mental retardation.

Health authorities throughout the United States responded to the news that PKU-retardation can be avoided when detected in time. Though births of children in families with known cases of phenylketonuria are watched with special care, most states now require that the urine of *all* hospital-born babies be tested for phenylpyruvic acid.

The discovery of the cause and the control of phenylketonuria meant more than saving only those children who would otherwise be maimed by this — fortunately — rare disease. It gave hope that other forms of mental retardation and mental illness might be traced to errors in metabolism. There seemed to be a good chance that, once such errors had been discovered, these conditions could be remedied by drug therapy or dietary measures.

And, indeed, scientists succeeded in their quest. A whole series of metabolic disorders of the PKU type has been discovered, in which mental retardation is one of the symptoms of faulty metabolism of amino acids. These, however, account for only a fraction of all mental retardation cases. The intellectual development of young children can be stunted by a host of conditions, such as infections, birth injury, mongolism, malnutrition, deprivation and many others, the exact nature of which is still unknown, since the precise cause of only 15 to 20 per cent of all cases of retardation are known today.

13 ALMOST HUMAN

Most medical discoveries owe a debt of gratitude to animals used in scientific experiments. Basically, animals reproduce, repair their tissues, transform food into flesh and energy, and react to chemical compounds in a remarkably similar manner, whether the animal is a man, a mouse, a monkey or an elephant.

Physically speaking, man is ill-equipped for survival. He is not fast like the deer or armed with strong claws; his teeth are not fangs like the wolf's, and he is not streamlined like a fish. He has no coat to protect him in winter, he cannot wing through the air, or swim across oceans, and yet — he is the undisputed master of the earth! He holds this unique position only because of one thing: his fantastically intricate brain.

His superior mental faculties, however, made man the only candidate for mental illness — or so it seemed until half a century ago. Since then, it has been demonstrated that under appropriate circumstances animals can become as neurotic as their human masters.

This fact, as well as most of what is known of the behavior and learning processes in animals, is an outgrowth of the work started toward the end of the last century by the Russian physiologist, Ivan Petrovich Pavlov. He studied the interrelationship between *messages received* from the outside and the *physiological response* of the body.

Pavlov investigated an organism's answer or *response* to a simple physical message, or *stimulus,* like food. When a newborn puppy is first given milk, its taste buds are stimulated, and saliva, necessary for digestion, starts flowing. This is an *unconditioned reflex;* the puppy's response was inborn, and it does not have to have any previous experience or knowledge to salivate. Rapidly, however, the puppy gets used to the sight and smell of milk, and its mouth waters as soon as it sees the experimenter approaching with the bowl. Its response — salivation — has now become a *conditioned reflex,* meaning that it depends on previously acquired experience.

To investigate this phenomenon further, Pavlov designed experiments in which, each time he fed one of his dogs, he would first ring a bell and then offer the food. After a number of repetitions of the exact procedure — same bell, same interval between sound and food — the dog's mouth would water whenever it heard the bell, even when no reward (food) was forthcoming. After a few days the dog associated the sound of the bell with food. The stimulation of the taste buds had been replaced by a *conditioned stimulus* (sound of the bell), and the message traveled over nerve pathways involving higher brain centers. (Such a process is, of course, not restricted to animals; we have only to think "lemon" for our mouths to water.)

At first, Pavlov, and many experimental physiologists and

psychologists who followed in his tracks, investigated only normal learning processes in man and beast. It quickly became apparent, however, that animals become confused and neurotic when confronted with frequent changes in experimental procedure, or frustrated when they are unable to differentiate between closely related stimuli. One of Pavlov's dogs, unable to tell the difference between a circle and an ellipse (he got a reward only when he responded to the circle), became so furious that he attacked and destroyed the test apparatus.

Pavlov was a contemporary of Freud, but whereas Freud's investigations were the object of much controversy, Pavlov's received recognition. Even prior to his turning to experimental psychology, he had made his scientific mark and, in 1904, had received the Nobel Prize for his work on the physiology of digestion. He was past fifty when he switched from digestion to conditioning, and not until he was eighty did he decide "to make closer acquaintance with psychiatry, of which almost no traces have remained in my memory since my student days in the medical faculty." He hoped to apply the skills gained in the treatment of his experimentally induced neuroses in animals to human patients. In part, as he told an American visitor in 1935, he was led to try these experiments by reading some of Freud's work.

Pneumonia, to which he succumbed a year later, put an end to the research of this tireless scientist who said of himself: "I am an experimenter from head to foot. My whole life has been given to experiment."

Dr. Jules Masserman, a psychiatrist presently working at Northwestern University in Chicago, also felt that much could be learned from experimentally induced neuroses.

Since the early 1930's, he and his colleagues have devoted part of their time to animal experimentation, working mostly with cats, dogs and monkeys.

Cats were first taught to operate an automatic feeding device which, after flashing a light and ringing a bell, delivered a breaded pellet of salmon. After a number of weeks, the automatic salmon pellet dispenser was so rigged that delivery of the fish was accompanied by a mild blast of air across the snout of the unsuspecting cat. The animal, though hungry, would retreat hastily, and after undergoing the same unpleasant experience a number of times, it refused to eat, was afraid of light, loud noises, closed spaces and even caged mice. Rapidly, its unhappy mental state permeated its entire life pattern. The cat could not get along with other cats, became overaggressive, incapable of mating, and also regressed to kittenish behavior and became overly dependent.

In another group of experiments, monkeys were also trained to operate an automatic feeding device. After a while, delivery of the food was accompanied by the appearance of a toy snake. Then the monkeys had to choose between two mutually exclusive patterns of survival: feeding when hungry, and avoiding snakes, for which they have an instinctive fear. As in the case of the cats, such conflicts resulted in well-defined neurotic behavior.

Since Masserman's main concern is the treatment of mental illness, he proceeded to institute "animal psychotherapy." As with man, the best results were obtained by kindness, friendly behavior, removal to a less stressful environment, slow retraining, encouragement to use previously learned skills and — very important — a trustful relationship with "the therapist."

Curiously enough, Masserman discovered that some of

his neurotic cats took a liking to alcohol, which seemed to help them overcome some of their anxieties.

While Masserman, the psychiatrist, deliberately set out to create neurotic animals, psychologists working at the nearby University of Wisconsin carried out experiments designed to investigate mother-infant relationships in monkeys.

Harry F. and Margaret Kuenne Harlow, a husband-and-wife team, needed some healthy, disease-free monkeys. They therefore separated baby monkeys permanently from their mothers a few hours after birth, and placed them in clean, individual cages, where they were provided with bottled milk and other creature comforts.

The infants grew into physically strong and healthy animals. As a matter of fact, there were fewer deaths among these bottle-fed monkey babies than among those nursed by their mothers. And yet, when fully grown, the behavior of fifty-six monkeys so raised was the weirdest anybody had ever seen. They did not play or frolic, as monkeys normally do, but acted like mental patients. They sat in a corner of the cage, stared fixedly into space, or walked in circles for hours. Some clasped their heads in their hands, others kept pinching the same patch of skin over and over again. When approached by man or monkey they became frightened, but, instead of attacking the intruder, they tore at their own coats or bit themselves. When fully grown and ready to mate, none of the animals was capable of normal courtship.

In the 1950's the Harlows, and other psychologists of Wisconsin's Primate Laboratory, embarked on an extensive monkey-raising program. They hoped by their investigation to be able to shed some additional light on Sigmund Freud's theories concerning the effect of early mother-infant and sibling relationships on the emotional development of the adult. So far, these had not been tested experimentally, for no one would deliberately expose a child to neglect and lack of love. Whatever conclusions Freud had come to were reached by working backward — that is, by examining the adult and, from his reactions and recollections, deducing in what manner he had been shaped by childhood experiences.

The Harlows' findings indicated that baby monkeys could perhaps serve as an adequate substitute. Like humans, they have a rather long childhood, and, furthermore, their mothers provide them with lavish care. Also, baby monkeys — like children — are playful creatures, in great need of playmates from an early age.

The monkey-raising experiments were designed to establish the difference between the influence of the mother and that of age-mates. In either set of experiments, the infants were separated from their mothers within hours after birth. This was necessary in order to reduce maternal protest to a minimum. Once a monkey mother has become used to her infant, it takes more than one person to force her to give it up.

Once separated, the infants were placed into a cage with one of two *surrogate* or "substitute" mothers. One was a bare, welded wire structure; the other "mother" was covered with soft terry cloth. Both "mothers" supplied their charges with a bottle of milk whose nipples protruded from their respective "breasts." Physiologically, both types of mothers proved equally good. Their infants grew strong and fat. Emotionally, however, they were quite different, the cloth-covered ones being infinitely more be-

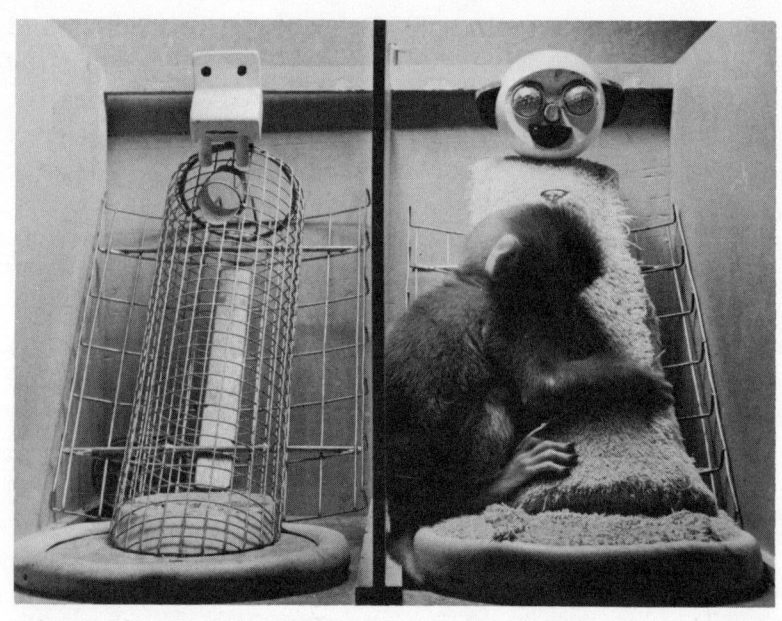

Baby monkey with two types of surrogate mothers.

loved. Their infants spent a large part of the day clinging to and climbing all over them, whereas the wire "mothers" received no attention except at feeding time. Later, when the monkeys had grown and were tested in a specially devised playpen, into which the experimenter had placed a series of unfamiliar objects, all the monkeys were very frightened, and crouched in the corners of their cages.

However, the monkeys which had been raised with a cloth "mother" were reassured when the latter was put into the playpen. Here the monkeys again acted like small children who are perfectly happy to explore a new place as long as their mother is present in the same room. Wire "mothers" provided their "offspring" with no such reassurance.

In some ways, the terry-cloth "mothers" appear to be better than real-life mothers; they have infinite patience, and never show any kind of displeasure. However, this lack of "rejection" proved no advantage. On the contrary, it meant that their infants never learned to venture forth alone. They also never learned to get along with other monkeys and to mate when old enough. They remained lonely, disturbed, social outcasts throughout life.

In spite of all kinds of difficulties, a few of the young "motherless" females became pregnant. When their infants

"Motherless" monkey.

were born, they proved to be most unsatisfactory mothers, constantly rejecting their infants, and even refusing to let them nurse. The young would surely have died outside of the protected atmosphere of the laboratory, where food for the babies was supplied by the experimenter. In spite of unsatisfactory mothering, the second-generation monkeys, however, acted more or less normally when grown up. It is, as yet, too early to tell whether they will be able to provide their offspring with affection.

In a second series of experiments, the Wisconsin group permitted four infant monkeys, raised without mothers, to socialize for about twenty minutes each day in a large common playroom. There they could frolic, climb, chase, swing, fight and cling together to their hearts' content. In spite of the complete absence of maternal care, and the brevity of their daily play period, these infants grew into normal adults, able to mate, play-fight and defend themselves. Surprisingly, they were much more normal than a similar group of monkeys raised with their natural mothers but without the companionship of age-mates. For monkeys, at least, social intercourse with "friends" of the same age appeared to be even more important than mothering.

When some of Wisconsin's disturbed monkeys were fully grown, an attempt was made to cure them by "group psychotherapy." Nineteen animals were taken to the monkey island of Madison's municipal zoo. Survival itself was a challenge here. Water no longer came in bottles, but had to be drunk from an open trough. The animals had to compete for food, huddle together for warmth, climb rocks and avoid the water surrounding the island. All but three animals succeeded in adapting physically to their new surroundings. They learned to live together, and established friendships, but never succeeded in mating. The "group therapy," however, had no lasting effect. Once back in the familiar atmosphere of the laboratory, they resumed their lonely, unhappy lives.

At about the time the Harlows investigated the effects of social deprivation on the development of monkeys, very similar conclusions were reached by a man working with children whom fate had deprived of their parents.

For a very long time orphans had been neglected and exploited. Charles Dickens' story of Oliver Twist is fiction, but truly appalling conditions existed in workhouses and similar institutions. The advent of social reforms changed the orphanages, and modern buildings, equipped with sanitary facilities, were built. Nurses and educators were provided, and kitchens were supervised by trained dietitians who saw to it that each child received a daily requirement of proteins and vitamins. Yet, in spite of all this perfection, most orphans reared in institutions never fitted into everyday society. They grew into lonely, dissatisfied men and women, incapable of meeting the demands of adult life.

Though the world has always had its share of homeless children, their numbers invariably multiply after each social upheaval. Throngs of orphaned or abandoned children were roaming through Eastern Europe after World War II, and they preyed on the mind of Hermann Gmeiner, a young Austrian medical student.

He had been motherless since the age of four. His father did not remarry and the oldest daughter, then only eighteen, kept house and cared for her seven younger brothers and sisters. From the age of twelve, however, Hermann was on his own. There was no high school in his native village, and to continue his education he had to stay in nearby Feldkirchen. Like Philippe Pinel, so many years earlier, he supported himself by tutoring in mathematics and Latin. On Sundays he served as an altar boy.

Gmeiner had decided to become a doctor, but by the time he was ready to start his training, the world was at war, and he was drafted into the German army. He spent the next five years at the Russian front. In 1945, he returned briefly to the family farm in Alberschwende and then entered the University of Innsbruck to study medicine and philosophy. Pediatrics was to be his specialty.

But the problems of the world at large, especially those of the orphans, kept troubling him. He felt that "these children had no chance of a normal upbringing in the ruined cities and large refugee camps of Europe." The existing, impersonal orphan asylums were no answer. As he said: "When we place a child who has just lost his mother or both parents in such an institution, we complete the process of writing the child out of our normal society."

At first, Gmeiner helped some children individually, while continuing to study, but when one of his charges committed suicide he closed his medical books for good. He knew mankind needed a new way of caring for its homeless young:

> Not life in an orphanage or any other kind of institution, no matter how "advanced," where the child was only a temporary charge (and knew it), but life in an ordinary house with a hearth, a living room, and a bedroom, where the child would live with a resident

"mother" and with other children, who would become his "brothers" and "sisters." The houses would be solid and comfortable, but not luxurious, corresponding to the homes of factory foremen and white-collar workers. A dozen or more such houses would form an SOS Children's Village.

Many kindhearted and idealistic citizens might have dreamt of such new ways of solving an old problem, but Gmeiner turned his vision into reality. In May, 1949, he took his "entire fortune" amounting to the equivalent of $42.00, knocked on the doors of neighbors and friends, and soon had enough money to build the first "SOS Children's Village," in Imst, Austria, which closely resembled his "dream."

Each home in the village houses a "mother," and a "family" of nine children, ranging in age from three days to eighteen years. The children go to a nearby public school, and family life in the SOS homes includes birthday parties, picnics, Christmas trees, as well as justly deserved punishments. Children, like monkeys, need both love and discipline to grow into responsible adults.

Though a mother, who has intimate knowledge of all her children, is the center of any family, the relationship between siblings can be equally important. Gmeiner describes one boy who had shown every sign of becoming a lifelong social outcast. He had been completely unmanageable in numerous institutions, and now even his "mother" in the Children's Village was about to give up. Just before the boy was to be placed in a home for delinquents, his "family" acquired a new baby girl. The boy immediately took a great liking to his new sister. He volunteered his help, ran errands, fetched and carried, and before long went about the village telling how good his "mother" was to his little sister.

Since the founding of the first Children's Village, in 1949, similar villages have sprung up in many parts of the world. As Gmeiner hoped and predicted, his "children" are much happier than those reared in large, impersonal orphanages.

The Children's Villages have added much to man's knowledge of child rearing. In a different way, they duplicate the discoveries of Harlows' group in Wisconsin. But growing up is a complicated process, and the fact that many children, reared by conscientious parents in loving homes, are ill-equipped to cope with the trials of everyday life is an indication that much remains to be discovered.

14 CHEMICALS COME TO THE RESCUE

*Behind every crooked thought there
lies a crooked molecule.*
— Ralph W. Gerard

For as long as he has been gathering food, man also must have been searching the earth for medicines to alleviate pain, cure fevers and bring the mad back to their senses. Greek mythology tells of a successful attempt to achieve the last, and perhaps the most difficult, of these tasks. Proetus was saddled with a pair of delinquent daughters who refused to marry, or honor the gods, and who stole gold from the statue of the goddess Hera. In retaliation, the gods deluded the girls into believing themselves to be cows. They left their father's palace and roamed wildly across the Peloponnesian peninsula of Greece. Their distressed father engaged the services of the seer Melampus, a wise and shrewd observer, who had noticed that the herb hellebore had a purgative effect on goats.

In those days illness, regardless of whether it affected the mind or the body, was believed to be caused by poisons or evil spirits, either of which had to be purged before health would return. Drugs that would induce vomiting or diarrhea were great favorites, and Melampus figured that what worked for goats might work for cows. He therefore fed hellebore to the royal cow-daughters, cured them of their madness, and in payment asked Proetus for two-thirds of his kingdom. His remedy, hellebore, became a widely

"The physician curing fantasy, also purging madness by drugs" (French School, seventeenth century). The apothecary jars on the shelves contain reason, virtue, intelligence, cheerfulness and the like.

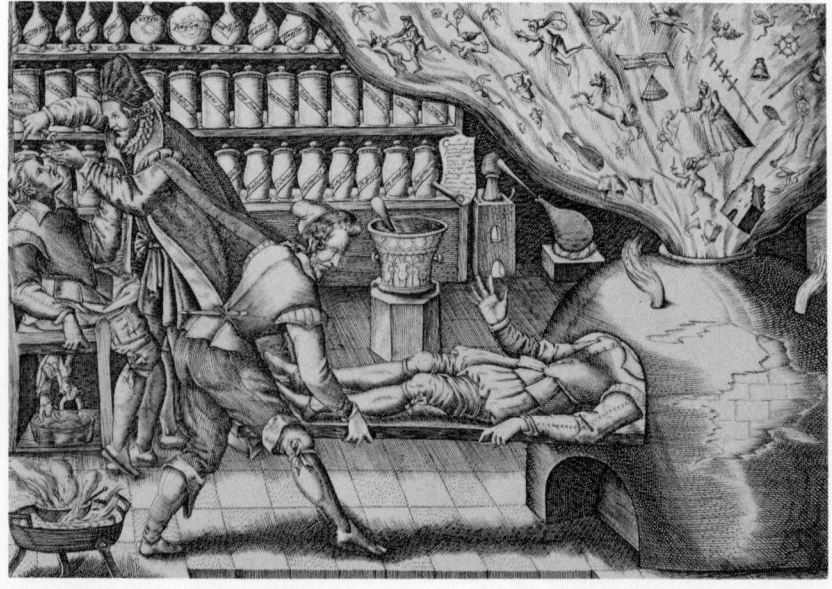

CHEMICALS COME TO THE RESCUE

used medicinal herb in ancient Greece, especially for diseases of the mind.

Hellebore was only one of many plant medicines used from ancient times in various parts of the world. There were: valerian, linden flowers, guaiac wood, nightshade, opium poppy, laurel leaves, sassafras, foxglove, cinchona bark and scores of others. Many proved later to be useless and are now quite forgotten. Others were so effective that they are still part of today's medicinal arsenal. Quinine, for instance, first extracted from cinchona bark and now man-made, is an excellent remedy for malaria, and digitalis, the active principle of foxglove, is widely prescribed today for certain heart conditions.

While some medicinal plants — good or bad — became important items of trade in the days of the caravans and sailing ships, others were completely unknown outside of their homelands. One of these was India's snakeroot plant. Though legend has it that the mongoose would nibble on its leaves to increase its strength before fighting a cobra, it was more likely named for its long, winding roots, as well as the fact that it was often used as an antidote for snakebite. It was also recommended for scorpion stings, epilepsy, dysentery, insomnia, blindness, cholera, diarrhea, insanity and to soothe fretful babies.

In 1703, the snakeroot plant acquired a scientific name: *Rauwolfia serpentina*. It was named by the French botanist Charles Plumier in memory of Leonhard Rauwolf, a German physician-explorer and botanist who had studied the medicinal plants of the Orient in 1573. But even with a new name, *Rauwolfia serpentina* remained unknown and almost forgotten until the 1920's, when its curative powers were investigated by several Indian scientists.

From the *Rauwolfia* roots, bought at a local bazaar, scientists extracted and purified five different *alkaloids* — complex chemical molecules, some of which have medicinal properties. Today many different medicinal alkaloids are extracted from the snakeroot plant; the most active one is called *reserpine*.

While *Rauwolfia serpentina* was being investigated in the laboratory, two other Indian physicians, Drs. Gananth Sen and Kartrick Chandra Bose, subjected the plant to medical scrutiny. After a few animal tests showed it to be safe, the drug was tried on man.

Announcements of discoveries that later prove to be turning points in medical history are often modest. The Indian doctors' scientific paper, entitled *Rauwolfia serpentina, A New Indian Drug for Insanity and High Blood Pressure*, reporting the results obtained with a powder made from the roots of the snakeroot plant was no exception:

> *Rauwolfia serpentina* is a drug of rare merit . . . with those who know the drug and use it in insanity, it is usually a precious and closely guarded secret. . . . The first author of this article traced it and identified the drug with some difficulty. Since then he has used it freely amongst his patients with remarkable success . . . [He] was fortunate in discovering the effect of the drug on blood pressure also, and he was able to regulate the blood pressure of his patients . . . almost to a precision not found possible with any other drug, Eastern and Western. . . .
>
> The authors have used it in all types of insanity and have found out that it is effective only in a certain type

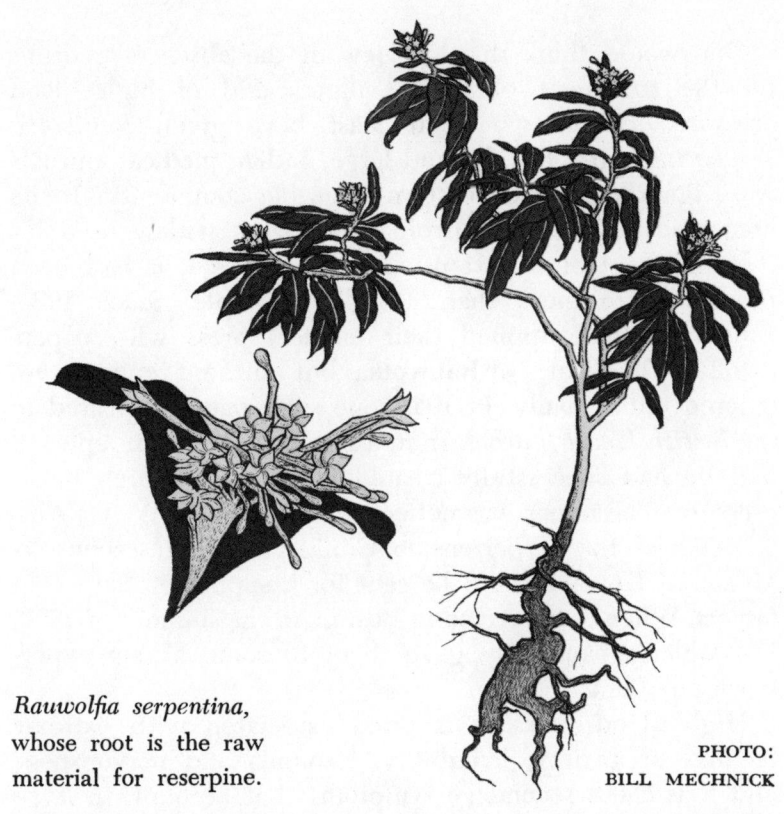

Rauwolfia serpentina, whose root is the raw material for reserpine.

PHOTO: BILL MECHNICK

of insanity which is common. Insanity with violent maniacal symptoms yields readily to it.

High blood pressure, also called hypertension, is common, especially in the aging. Since, on the average, man lives longer today than he did years ago, the treatment of hypertension is becoming an increasingly important problem of medicine, and one for which no effective medication existed in 1930.

One would think that, in view of the absence of drugs for the treatment of mental illness and of high blood pressure, doctors would at least have given *Rauwolfia serpentina* a try, but, by and large, Indian medical journals were ignored by the Western scientific community. In its homeland, however, Rauwolfia was being widely used for the treatment of hypertension, and, by 1944, it had been prescribed to more than a million people. Since 1930, Indian doctors supplied their medical press with papers extolling the virtues of Rauwolfia, but all these reports were ignored until, finally, in 1949, one such paper appeared in the *British Heart Journal.* In it, a Bombay physician reported that he had successfully treated fifty cases of high blood pressure. The paper was noticed by Dr. Robert W. Wilkins, Director of the Hypertension Clinic at the Massachusetts Memorial Hospitals, and he sent for a supply of Rauwolfia tablets. When they arrived in Boston, in the summer of 1950, Dr. Wilkins cautiously gave them to some of his hypertensive patients.

High blood pressure is often associated with extreme feelings of anxiety, irritability, insomnia and nervousness, and it is these secondary symptoms that account, in large part, for the misery of the patient. To Wilkins' delight, Rauwolfia not only lowered blood pressure, it also made his patients feel "as if they simply didn't have a worry in the world."

Surprisingly, in spite of Rauwolfia's age-old reputation as a drug for the treatment of insanity, another few years passed before it was tried in cases of severe mental illness. Perhaps those in charge of the large state institutions, housing thousands of patients, had been disappointed too often by false promises.

The monkey on the right, who was treated with barbiturates (sleeping pills), is unconscious. His companion, who received a dose of reserpine, is calm but alert.

Since Pinel took charge of the wards of the Salpêtrière in 1798, conditions in mental hospitals had become more humane, but had the lot of the severely disturbed really improved? Every mental hospital still had its hopeless "back wards" full of patients who had been there for decades, patients who would not remain clothed, patients who would not talk or talked unceasingly, patients bent on destroying their lives, patients terrified by imaginary mon-

167

sters, patients who believed they were George Washington, Jesus Christ or the Virgin Mary.

Every available method of treatment had been tried on them without lasting success. Their illness had persisted through electroshock and insulin treatments; they were much too ill even to be approached by psychoanalysis. Prolonged sleep therapy, carbon dioxide and Metrazol treatment, as well as other promising methods had come and gone, but the patients had remained a burden to themselves, their families, those responsible for their well-being, and objects of fear to all of humanity.

Sooner or later, however, every new method of treatment is given a chance, and so it was with *Rauwolfia serpentina*. Among the first to experiment with it were two psychiatrists working at Modesto State Hospital in California. They tried Rauwolfia on 74 patients, then on 247 more. These were all severe and "hopeless" cases; most were schizophrenics. A few patients had received more than 100 electroshock treatments, and many came from the maximum security wards.

It was almost as if Rauwolfia worked magic. Within two months, the noisy, restless, nightmarish wards, where attendants constantly had to use force, had become quiet and almost cheerful. Suddenly, some patients wanted to work, went to the dining room, benefited from psychotherapy and many could even be sent home!

Evidence of the effectiveness of reserpine (Rauwolfia's most active alkaloid) kept pouring in from New York, Iowa, Maryland, Illinois, Louisiana and Washington, D.C. The verdict was unanimous. Reserpine was the best thing ever to happen to the mentally ill. True, it did not "cure" mental illness the way penicillin cures bacterial infections,

CHEMICALS COME TO THE RESCUE

for when the drug was discontinued the symptoms returned. Also, it was not effective for every type of mental illness, but it helped a great many people to live normal, productive lives.

While nature's gift to the insane was fighting an uphill battle for recognition, scientists were busy preparing and testing new man-made drugs. The development of new medicines is a complicated process. Hundreds of new compounds are tested every year and, at best, a few may prove useful. A chemist searching for a new drug is very much like an artist trying out a new combination of colors and textures, shapes and forms. The chemist, like the artist, tries to combine "something new with something old," something that has worked before with a modification that might make it a more powerful drug — or one with fewer side effects, because often the side effects limit a drug's usefulness. An effective medicine may be too toxic; it may cause nausea, dizziness, or even damage to unborn children.

In 1952, chemists at the Rhône-Poulenc Laboratories in France were looking for a better antihistamine drug. The antihistamine preparations are effective for controlling asthma and allergies. Unfortunately, they often cause so much drowsiness that persons taking antihistamines are cautioned against driving. One of the new "antihistamines" the French scientists believed would cause less drowsiness was R.P. 4560.

Testing new drugs is always difficult. Fortunately, scientists have learned how to "give" many human diseases to certain members of the animal kingdom. Ferrets can "get" flu; mice, yellow fever; monkeys, polio; chickens and hamsters, cancer.

But testing certain kinds of drugs in animals presents special problems. How was one to determine whether R.P. 4560, for example, made a rat or a dog less drowsy than one of its sister compounds, especially since the sleeping pattern of most animals is so different from that of man? Normally, dogs like to nap anytime they can, yet they are ready to eat or go for a walk twenty-four hours a day. When they are medicated with sedatives or hypnotics (sleeping pills) or antihistamines, their behavior changes. After being roused, they remain sleepy and groggy and even food does not get the usual enthusiastic response.

Reaction to R.P. 4560 was different from the reaction to previously tested antihistamines, sedatives or hypnotics. Though it induced sleep, the dogs, when wakened, were alert and in full possession of their "dog sense."

The next clue that R.P. 4560 was special came from rats. Psychologists devote countless hours training rats to run mazes, press buzzers and perform many similar tasks. The rat's reward is food, and the scientist's a better understanding of learning processes. But scientists also like to study "frustration," and to this end they deprive the animal of a reward. When this happens, the rat becomes anxious, confused and upset, and its behavior approximates that observed in certain mental illnesses.

After R.P. 4560 had proved so interesting in the dogs, it was fed to "frustrated" rats. Anxiety and neurotic behavior vanished; the animals were completely "tranquilized." They had also forgotten all the tricks (conditioned reflexes) they had learned. Now R.P. 4560 became Rhône-Poulenc's most urgent business. The compound's potential use as a better antihistamine was forgotten, and it was tried on unmanageable mental patients.

From here the story of chlorpromazine — R.P. 4560's pharmaceutical name — reads like the story of reserpine. Within a matter of months, chlorpromazine had freed hundreds of mentally ill of their panic, fear, hostility, agitation, and the accompanying aggressive, assaultive and destructive behavior. It also had lessened their hallucinations and delusions. "It was," as one patient said after a short course of treatment with the new drug, "like a chairman taking control of a meeting where previously everybody had been shouting at once."

Perhaps the most encouraging thing was that chlorpromazine did not duplicate the action of reserpine. Some patients profited more from one drug than from the other, and some were helped by a combination of the two.

As soon as the wards were quieted by tranquilizers, psychiatrists began to hope and search for another type of drug — one that would help their depressed, melancholic patients to emerge from their feelings of grief. In addition, such a drug might provide the patients with more energy for intellectual and physical activity, improve their appetite and decrease their need for sleep.

As in the case of chlorpromazine, help came from a drug developed for another purpose. *Iproniazid*, another man-made drug, had been used successfully in the treatment of tuberculosis. Iproniazid, together with two other compounds, had emptied the nation's TB hospitals of many of their patients. One of the side effects of this drug was that it improved the mood of the tubercular patients to such an extent that they often believed themselves well sooner than they actually were, and this led them to discontinue medication before they were completely cured.

Iproniazid had been given to patients who suffered both

from tuberculosis and depression, but their marked mental improvement had been overlooked in the noisy wards where the attendants had to devote most of their energies to calm down disruptive patients. In due time, however, these side effects were recognized and studied by Dr. Nathan S. Kline, Director of Research at New York's Rockland State Hospital, and it turned out that psychiatrists had the *psychostimulant* drugs they had been seeking.

The discovery of these early tranquilizers and stimulants opened a new field of research: *psychopharmacology* — or the treatment of the mind by medicines. It is a big and fast-growing field. Today, dozens of tranquilizers and stimulants are on the market, and their use is not restricted to those who are mentally ill. Miltown and Librium (called minor tranquilizers) are prescribed for neuroses and other conditions in which emotional factors play an important role, and, currently, many psychiatrists use drugs in conjunction with psychotherapy.

Often, when there are many drugs instead of only one, it means that the perfect medication for the illness has not yet been discovered, or that the same drug does not benefit all patients. This is certainly true of mental disorders caused by a variety of factors requiring many different methods of treatment.

Ten years before chlorpromazine was synthesized in the laboratories of Rhône-Poulenc in France, a chemist, Dr. Albert Hofmann, working in nearby Switzerland, made a chance discovery that proved very interesting to those trying to understand the workings of the mind.

One day, when Dr. Hofmann was working with the

alkaloids of ergotamine — another long-known plant drug — he accidentally inhaled or swallowed a minute amount of the compound. Recalling later the sensations of this first LSD "trip" Dr. Hofmann wrote in his notebook:

> Last Friday, the 16th of April, I had to leave my work in the laboratory and go home because I felt strangely restless and dizzy. Once there, I lay down and sank into a not unpleasant delirium which was marked by an extreme degree of fantasy. In a sort of trance with closed eyes (I found the daylight unpleasantly glaring) fantastic visions of extraordinary vividness accompanied by a kaleidoscopic play of intense coloration continuously swirled around me. After two hours this condition subsided.

Dr. Hofmann attributed these strange sensations to the toxic effects of the substance he was working with, LSD — short for lysergic acid diethylamide — a degradation product of ergotamine. To make sure, Hofmann deliberately took 250 micrograms (one-quarter of a milligram) of the drug. Again, as he wrote in his notebook, he suffered from blurred vision, uncontrollable laughter, dizziness and an inability to concentrate. It became clear that LSD belongs to a class of drugs known as hallucinogenic agents. In certain doses, they produce symptoms that simulate those in psychoses.

Unfortunately, LSD has left the scientific laboratory and has become a hazard to those bent on playing with their sanity. It has caused permanent mental illness, has made sane and happy people commit suicide, and has induced others to commit murder. Recent evidence has also shown that, like excess radiation, LSD may cause chromosome breakage and that parents who have taken LSD are more likely to have babies with severe birth defects.

Continuing laboratory research with LSD may, in the end, solve the riddle of some mental disorders. Perhaps a "metabolic error," like the one found in PKU, produces an LSD-like chemical that prevents man's mind from functioning properly. So far, however, no clear-cut biochemical difference has been found between normal and schizophrenic persons. Meanwhile, until scientists discover a way of curing mental disease, physicians gratefully rely in large measure on a variety of mental drugs that finally have freed most patients of the chains Pinel and others began to cut more than 250 years ago.

15 GROUP THERAPY

> Joseph Hersey Pratt: 1872-1949
> Samuel R. Slavson: 1891-
> William Claire Menninger: 1899-1966

Medicine has grown so rapidly in recent times that it is hard to believe that a mere half-century ago doctors were almost as helpless in the face of many diseases as they were in the days of Hippocrates. One such disease was tuberculosis, or "consumption." Today, fortunately, most victims of TB can be cured by recently discovered drugs, but in 1905, when Dr. Joseph Hersey Pratt was in charge of tubercular patients at the Massachusetts General Hospital in Boston, no effective medication was available. The only recourses a physician had were the healing power of nature and plenty of crisp mountain air.

In America many tubercular patients were sent to hospitals and sanatoria located in the Adirondacks, Colorado and other highlands. But not everyone could afford the cost, and many had to remain in the slums of the rapidly expanding cities. It was for these that Pratt organized his now historical "Classes for the Treatment of Tuberculosis in the Homes of the Poor." The doctor had come to the conclusion that plenty of fresh city air was better than no fresh air at all, and he wanted to teach his patients how to make the most of the meager resources of city dwellers: parks, backyards, roofs and porches.

Group therapy session.

GROUP THERAPY

In order to save valuable time, Pratt assembled a group of patients once a week for a pleasant social hour, during which he lectured on the importance of continuing their therapy. Then he turned the floor over to "the class." One by one, the patients would report on how they had solved their common problem: some had pitched tents in backyards, others on roofs; fire escapes had been converted into porches, and one patient who had been denied even the use of the fire escape told of how he slept with his head sticking out of the window. The rate of recovery of the participants was remarkably high, as high as that obtained at Saranac Lake in the Adirondacks and at other first-class sanatoria. The pleased physician concluded that this success could not be due entirely to the improvised methods of treatment but must, to a large extent, be attributed to the interaction of the group itself, which provided each patient with a "common bond in a common disease."

According to Richard C. Cabot, a fellow physician who had occasion to watch the progress of this first group, here was "the truth, but not the whole truth," because he thought that Pratt in his evaluation had underestimated the power of his own dynamic and likable personality. In Cabot's opinion, the success and improvement of the patients was due "not wholly because they wanted to get well, but largely because he [Pratt] wanted them to — a very queer and very human state of things."

Be that as it may, Pratt was sufficiently impressed by the success of this class that, for the next fifty years, he devoted part of his professional time to the treatment of several types of disorders by *group therapy*. As an internist, he was most concerned with organic diseases, such as diabetes, but he also organized groups for patients with

Family group therapy gives a person with mental problems, and other members of his family, an understanding of the situation, which may mean a long step toward recovery.

nervous disorders. In these group sessions, he would deliberately ask his patients to talk about their worrisome thoughts.

More than other new forms of treatment, group therapy evolved, almost by accident, from a number of different settings. One of the early pioneers was Samuel R. Slavson. In 1911, he had abandoned a career in civil engineering to devote himself to education. The building of healthy personalities, he felt, was much more valuable as well as more interesting than fashioning concrete roads and steel bridges.

At first, his main interest was to help deprived youngsters to discover and develop their hidden talents. Musical education, literature and arts and crafts played an important role in his school and after-school programs. He organized a recreational group of this nature for children receiving psychiatric treatment at the Jewish Board of Guardians — an organization that operates several children's guidance clinics in New York City.

During their weekly meetings, Slavson's young charges did not produce any major works of art, nor did they seem to pay a great deal of attention to their creations, but after they participated in such a group for a number of months, their "teacher" could see that many of them had benefited immensely from these get-togethers. Slavson and his associates then devoted a great deal of time in an effort to determine what, exactly, had brought about the remarkable improvement. It was due, they concluded, to factors similar to those operating in individual Freudian analysis: positive transference, modification of old conflicts and acquiring of insight. Under the guidance of the therapist, the children had been able to release some of their feelings of resentment and hostility, and to express them. They had become more acceptable and accepting, and were better equipped to deal with the reality group situations of everyday life.

Slavson was even more impressed than Pratt with the unexpected healing power of a group, and he devoted himself fully to the study of group dynamics and interactions, and the means of shaping these forces into a new therapeutic tool. He and his associates experimented with many different kinds of groups designed for children of various ages and suffering from a variety of psychological problems and personality disorders. Soon he also established groups for the treatment of the parents of his young patients. Often, the child's problem is a symptomatic reflection of the emotional difficulties in his family, and real progress toward better understanding takes place only when the interrelationship among all family members becomes less hostile and more open.

Pratt, Slavson and many others made steady progress in their chosen field. However, group psychotherapy did not really come of age until World War II, when the U.S. Army was faced with the formidable task of caring for the mental and emotional well-being of eight million soldiers, more than 300,000 of whom were eventually to be discharged as psychiatric casualties.

Prior to 1942, the Army did not treat soldiers suffering from mental disorders; the job of its total staff of thirty-five psychiatrists was restricted to transferring such cases as quickly as possible to civilian medical care. But necessity, and the right man in the right job at the right time, were to change this practice. The man, William Claire Menninger, was a native of Topeka, Kansas.

His father, Charles Frederick Menninger, had settled in Topeka in the 1890's. He was a physician who even then believed that consultation, the exchange of medical views between doctors, could often lead to better medicine. Small Midwestern towns had too few physicians to make group practice a reality, and so "Dr. C. F.," as he was called, had to rely mostly on his own judgment. In time, however, two of his three sons, Karl Augustus and William Claire, went East to learn their father's profession. Karl,

Dr. William C. Menninger

the eldest, was first, and he specialized in psychiatry at Harvard University. Then he returned home and joined forces with his father. Together they treated a great many patients, though each man had his own specialty. Dr. C. F.'s was diabetes, Dr. Karl's was psychiatry. Gradually, however, the psychiatric cases won out, and the Menninger

Clinic became one of America's leading institutions for the care of the mentally ill.

At Harvard, Karl Menninger had learned little of the controversial methods of treating neurotic patients developed by Freud in Vienna. Surprisingly, it was one of his patients who first told him of psychoanalysis. A thorough study of the literature convinced him that the new method had possibilities, and he decided to go to Chicago for postgraduate training in psychiatry and a personal analysis.

By this time, William Claire, or "Dr. Will," had joined the family "group practice" as a general practitioner. But he too left Kansas and, to specialize in psychiatry, visited the world's great psychiatric centers in Zurich, Paris, London and Vienna, completing his training at the Institute for Psychoanalysis in Chicago.

Until 1925, the Menningers had hospitalized their patients at Christ Hospital in Topeka, but that institution, like most general hospitals, accepted mental cases with great reluctance, and that year the Menningers decided to buy a farm on the outskirts of town and convert it into a sanatorium. It was a small beginning, as only twelve patients could be accommodated. Slowly, however, the reputation of the hospital and of the Menningers grew, and, eventually, Topeka became one of the world centers of psychiatry, training 15 per cent of all North American psychiatrists, before World War II.

Peaceful growth in Kansas and elsewhere was shattered on December 7, 1941, when the Japanese bombed Pearl Harbor. It was logical for Dr. Will, the youngest of the Menninger team, to come to the aid of his country. In 1942, he became Neuropsychiatric Consultant to the Fourth Army Command, located in Atlanta, Georgia.

Luck, perseverance and an interest in stamp collecting, which he shared with his commanding officer, enabled William Menninger to change the kind of psychiatry practiced by the Fourth Army Command. Instead of simply transferring mental casualties into civilian hands, he saw to it that the soldiers in his charge received treatment in the Army.

Dr. Will did not stay long with the Fourth Army Command. In 1943, the former military Chief Psychiatrist died of a heart attack. Because of the reputation he had built up in Atlanta, Doctor Will received orders to report to Washington, where he became Chief Psychiatric Consultant to the Surgeon General of the U.S. Army. Thus a man who believed in the teachings and methods of Sigmund Freud — still subject to controversy — assumed the responsibility for the mental well-being of the entire U.S. armed forces.

Dr. Will was ideally suited for the job. He was not only an experienced and conscientious physician, but also a gifted organizer and a talented leader. In his youth, he had been a member of Boy Scout Troop Number 2 of Topeka, and for him "pathfinding" and "serving" had evolved into a way of life. The man, who in the past had often deferred to the counsel and leadership of his father and elder brother, had become the senior member of the Army's psychiatric team.

His problems were manifold, but basically they centered on recruiting and training sufficient medical personnel, and on developing methods suitable for the treatment of thousands of patients. Obviously, the individual treatment methods Dr. Will had used at the Menninger Clinic could not be used in the Army. New ways had to be found to alleviate the group anxiety caused by war. Soldiers were not only scarred physically by the ferocity of modern weapons, they were also emotionally crippled by fear and by the horrors they had witnessed. Just as it was necessary to remove a piece of shrapnel quickly from their wounds before they started to fester, it was imperative to attempt to relieve them also of their mental trauma.

The Army instituted psychiatric first-aid stations as close to the theaters of war as possible. There, psychiatrists asked battle-fatigued soldiers, suffering from a variety of hysterical and anxiety states, to recount their recent experiences. The patients were either hypnotized or put to sleep with narcotics. In the ensuing peculiar mental twilight, the soldiers were able to unburden themselves of some of the causes of their distress. The results far exceeded medical expectations, and many of the men, who otherwise would have been unfit for battle, returned to their posts within a short time.

Hypnotherapy and *narcotherapy*, as these procedures are called, have by now become part of psychiatry's ever-growing therapeutic arsenal. They are not used too extensively. The experience gained in the use of group therapy, however, was the Army's main gift to the treatment of mental disorders.

The shortage of therapists made it impossible for each patient to receive individual psychotherapy. Consequently, fifteen to twenty-five men were grouped together to talk about their problems. It quickly became obvious that, far from inhibiting exchanges, the group atmosphere encouraged the patients to talk more freely of experiences that they might have been unable to discuss in individual interviews. Discussion of current problems quite naturally

GROUP THERAPY

led to the recollection of childhood memories, and the consequent discovery that feelings of guilt and shame were not as unique as expected. This gave each man the strength Pratt had observed long before when he saw that his patients profited from their "common bond in a common disease."

Of course such an impersonal, mass-therapeutic approach was not suitable for everyone treated. Some patients felt neglected, others were even harmed. But time told the final story: Never before had such a large number of mentally and emotionally sick people been treated so successfully.

The Army not only provided psychiatry with new methods of treatment; it also built for postwar America a reservoir of action-trained psychiatrists. Many of those who had entered the medical corps had barely finished a general internship, and knew little about treating soldiers suffering from emotional disturbances. The doctors assigned to Psychiatric Service received some specialized training in hastily set-up instruction centers, but mostly they learned by doing, and often emergency became a great teacher. Since group therapy was the only feasible form of treatment, hundreds of young physicians learned more about group dynamics within a couple of months than they would have in a lifetime at home. When they returned to civilian life, many chose psychiatry as their specialty.

Partly because of the experience gained during the war, and partly because it is very effective, group therapy is assuming an increasingly important role in the treatment of persons with emotional problems. The various methods of group treatment presently used are as numerous as the disturbances they try to alleviate. There are lecture-oriented groups of the type Pratt used in Boston, in which the group leader plays a dominant role. There are activity groups of the kind Slavson developed at the Jewish Board of Guardians that use a common type of activity for therapeutic purposes. There are analytic groups, restricted to discussion and self-examination, in which each patient is helped to face his own resistance. Often, he might use his peers within the group to act out problems that had hindered him in his daily functioning.

Group therapy, however, is not restricted to people suffering from emotional problems. There are groups in which members, having rid themselves of a self-destructive habit like alcoholism, or drug addiction, help others to shake off this bondage. There are groups for the overweight; for adolescents and high school dropouts; for those who have to solve a common problem like bringing up children "without partners." And there are groups for business executives, psychiatrists, teachers and others whose professional activity requires self-examination and self-knowledge.

The Army, of course, could not return to its former state of indifference toward the mentally ill. At the end of the hostilities, fifty-five percent of the veterans were emotionally disturbed and would need care for years to come. Modern psychiatric hospitals were constructed, but new buildings would be of little use without experienced personnel. To obtain assistance, those in charge went to Topeka to see Dr. Will, who had served the nation so well in time of war.

Karl and Will Menninger agreed to help. As a first step, they converted the Menninger Clinic into the nonprofit Menninger Foundation. Instead of training three or four psychiatric residents a year, they now were training 100, or one-third of the total number of psychiatrists trained in the United States. Also, within a short time the Veteran's Administration Hospital in Topeka had become a model institution serving as a pattern for hospitals across America.

Dr. Will, however, felt that he could no longer devote himself exclusively to the Menninger Foundation, even though its responsibilities had multiplied a hundredfold since its beginning in 1919. Gradually, he became the spokesman for the mentally ill. Not since the days of Dorothea Dix, more than a hundred years earlier, had one person spoken to so many on behalf of those who could not speak for themselves. Like the schoolteacher from Massachusetts, he took his fight to the politicians of the land, and before he was through had addressed more than half of the state legislatures in the United States. On February 8, 1962, he was invited to the White House to put the cause of the mentally ill before President John F. Kennedy.

16 "THE TIME HAS COME FOR A BOLD NEW APPROACH"

— John F. Kennedy

Two health problems . . . are deserving of a wholly new national approach . . . These twin problems are mental illness and mental retardation . . . They occur more frequently, affect more people, require more prolonged treatment, cause more suffering by the families of the afflicted, waste more of our human resources, and constitute more financial drain upon both the public Treasury and the personal finances of the individual families than any other single condition . . . The time has come for a bold new approach . . . We must seek out the causes of mental illness and of mental retardation and eradicate them. Here, more than in any other area, "an ounce of prevention is worth more than a pound of cure." I am convinced that if we apply our medical knowledge and social insights fully, all but a small portion of the mentally ill can eventually achieve a wholesome and constructive social adjustment. It has been demonstrated that two out of three schizophrenics — our largest category of mentally ill — can be treated and released within six months, but under the conditions that prevail today the average stay for schizophrenia is eleven years . . . We need a new type of health facility, one which will return mental health care to the mainstream of American medicine . . .

— John F. Kennedy
February 5, 1963

Finally, after centuries of persecution, indifference, ignorance and neglect, medicine's stepchildren had achieved national prominence. The President had spoken and his words were not empty promises; they were backed by what Dorothea Dix had fought for in vain: Federal dollars, specifically earmarked for the development of new types of health facilities, such as community health centers; the improvement of state mental institutions; more prenatal and maternal care in order to reduce the incidence of mental retardation; special schools for the mentally deficient; and basic research to "seek out the causes of mental illness and mental retardation." The money would not be adequate to overcome all the hurdles, but it was more than had ever been available before.

One of the President's specific recommendations was that psychiatric patients be treated in special units of general community hospitals, so as to avoid a wide gulf between the mentally ill and the mentally well. It was felt that mental illness would lose some of its stigma if patients who needed hospitalization went to the same place as they would for surgery, childbirth or other conditions requiring temporary bed care.

Picnic area at the Mesa Vista Psychiatric Center in San Diego, California.

Some general hospitals had always accepted a few psychiatric cases, but the trend increased after World War II, and, by 1963, about 600 general hospitals had special psychiatric units. Spurred by federal funds, a few of these grew into major centers providing opportunities for testing whether treatment of mental illness, within the framework of a general hospital, would improve the chances of recovery of the patient and shorten his hospital stay.

One general hospital that has such facilities is Mount Sinai, in New York City. By mental hospital standards, Mount Sinai's psychiatric unit is small. It has 132 beds compared with thousands in many state institutions. That is not surprising, because general hospitals are not intended to treat, or house, the long-term custodial cases that make up the bulk of the state hospitals' population.

The spirit animating most of present-day medicine prevails in Mount Sinai's psychiatric unit: a massive attack on the problem at hand by the best available methods. In the case of acute mental breakdowns, the treatment is chiefly a combination of psychopharmacology and psychotherapy.

Since they were first discovered, less than fifteen years ago, the psychoactive drugs have multiplied, and today psychiatrists prescribe dozens of tranquilizers, energizers, antidepressants and other mind and mood modifiers. So effective are these drugs that methods of shock therapy, which seemed so promising only twenty years ago, are used as little as possible. At Mount Sinai, electroshock therapy, or EST, the most prevalent method, is used very rarely and very sparingly, primarily for severely depressed and suicidal patients who fail to respond to drug therapy. And, instead of the usual course of a dozen or more shock treatments, three to four seem to be sufficient. After that, such patients can also be "carried" on drugs.

Psychoactive drugs not only opened the locked doors of the mental hospital, they also make a disturbed patient more readily accessible to psychotherapy. Most of Mount Sinai's staff favors psychoanalysis. They believe that mental illness and social maladjustment are due to emotional conflicts that have to be at least partially resolved before a patient can successfully face the trials and pressures of everyday life.

At Mount Sinai this approach represents the central core of its everyday activities. Upon hospital admission each case is assigned to an individual doctor. As soon as the patient is able and ready, usually within a few days, he meets with his doctor daily, for a half-hour to an hour, to explore his inner self. These psychotherapeutic sessions are used to air the accumulated feelings of anger, fear and frustration, and to try and provide the patient with some self-knowledge and inner understanding. Daily living can be very much like running an obstacle course, with emotional conflicts looming like traps and stumbling blocks, and "insight" is like a torch with which it is possible to pick one's path more productively.

At Mount Sinai, as elsewhere, individual psychotherapy is supplemented by group psychotherapy. Patients are selected so that they may benefit from the group situation. They meet with one or two physicians and social workers to explore further their feelings, and to learn, or relearn, how to function in a group, first inside and eventually outside the hospital.

Individual and group therapy do not occupy all of the patient's time. The library provides books, the music room records and instruments, the recreation and social departments organize games, dances and other social activities, and the occupational therapy, or "O.T." department, supplies paints, clay and other arts and crafts materials.

Almost two centuries earlier, Benjamin Rush had observed that mental patients who participated in the maintenance work of the hospital fared better than those whose only company were their fantasies and morbid thoughts. He usually provided patients, who were well enough, with something to "occupy" themselves: knitting, gardening or

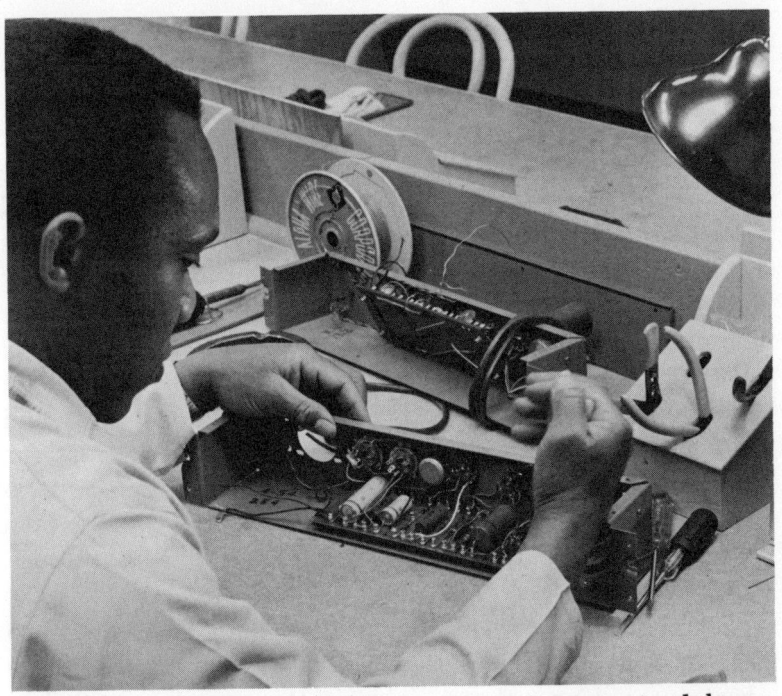

Patient disassembling a transmitter during occupational-therapy session.

even putting down their thoughts and fears on paper. Today O.T. is no longer used merely to give a patient "something to do." Creative art is a form of self-expression used extensively by psychotherapists who work with children. But even adults often reveal their feelings and conflicts more easily in a painting than in words or gestures. Thus art is another avenue of exploring the patient's inner problems and helping him gain insight and understanding.

The art work of a psychiatric patient is also an indicator of his state of mind and feelings. Initially, a newly admitted patient may paint a violent collection of blobs and colors which reflect his inner torment and disorganization. As the patient begins to recover, his paintings gradually become more controlled and meaningful.

Great care is taken at Mount Sinai to impress upon the patient the fact that he is ill and that he is in a medical hospital for treatment and recovery. Physically, the halls with their pajama-clad patients and uniformed nurses, look like those of any ordinary, well-appointed hospital, the only difference being a smaller number of the very old and a relatively larger number of young adults. Bed space at Mount Sinai, as in most hospitals, is in short supply, and only those patients who are most likely to profit from the intensive care are admitted. Patients requiring long-term care are not accepted, and younger patients, for whom psychotherapeutic treatment has always proved most successful, may receive preference.

The close link between the world of the ill and the world of the well that prevails at the hospital is further emphasized by four ordinary looking classrooms identified as "Mount Sinai Annex P.S. 368 K." Here all the children carry on their schooling, under the direction of specially trained teachers. Today mental illness, serious enough to require hospitalization, seems no longer sufficient reason to deprive children of their schooling.

At Mount Sinai talk is not restricted to verbal interchanges between patients and doctors. Part of the day is reserved for staff conferences, at which all those who are in contact with the patient discuss their observations and findings, and decide on what changes, if any, are to be made in the treatment process. Each psychiatric team includes a *caseworker* whose job is to visit the patient's family in order to determine to what extent his surroundings may have contributed to his illness. An attempt is made to help achieve a friendlier relationship within the family so that it can be more understanding and tolerant of the ailing member when he returns home.

The average hospital stay for psychiatric patients is from four to ten weeks. After that period, three-quarters of those admitted are well enough to return home, and the rest are transferred to various other institutions.

But care does not cease with discharge. Most patients return to the hospital as after-care patients for a weekly psychotherapy session with "their" doctor. Drug therapy is also continued for as long as it is deemed necessary. But even when the after-care sessions come to an end, the bond between Mount Sinai and its former patients is not completely severed. Anytime the patient feels that the demands of the outside world are becoming too strenuous he can return — with no waiting period — to "talk things over," to receive drug therapy and perhaps additional psychotherapy. Such an arrangement is important, for today "waiting for therapy" is becoming an increasingly pressing problem.

This growing need for additional mental health facilities is, however, only another aspect of medicine's shift from "repair" to anticipation and prevention. Today emotional and developmental problems can be spotted by trained psychologists and guidance counsellors who administer various psychological tests. These tests are used to determine a student's intellectual endowment, or lack of it, and serve as guidelines to proper scholastic placement, as well as pinpointing more accurately the disturbed student and planning for his treatment. Unfortunately, the number of available professionals is inadequate and teachers as well as students suffer from lack of special schools, and the paucity of diagnostic and mental health facilities.

One condition, estimated to affect five million children in the United States, which has been misdiagnosed and thus mishandled until recently, is minimal brain dysfunction — resulting from minor brain damage most frequently incurred at birth. Though many of these children are endowed with superior intelligence, they have great difficulties in learning certain specific tasks: spelling, reading, counting, catching a ball and walking along a chalk line. These seemingly minor difficulties rapidly mushroom into major ones: social isolation, emotional turmoil, disruptive behavior . . . heartache, failure and sometimes even lifetime institutionalization. Here, as elsewhere in medicine, "an ounce of prevention is worth a pound of cure," and most of these problems are avoided when such youngsters are taught in special schools, by teachers who provide instruction suited to the need of each student.

Careful distinctions have to be made in the case of very young children, whose therapy and treatment will depend on whether they are found to be mentally retarded or emotionally disturbed.

Psychiatry has always suffered from a lack of clear-cut diagnostic tests, which is not surprising. It is relatively easy to describe an illness in terms of fever, pulse rate, blood pressure, blood counts, blood sugar levels, the presence or absence of certain microorganisms and a variety of other concrete, measurable items. But an illness, manifesting itself by violent temper outbursts, day-long silence and withdrawal, sullenness or attempts at suicide, is much harder

"THE TIME HAS COME FOR A BOLD NEW APPROACH"

to characterize, especially since so much depends on the judgment of the therapist.

Recently, however, in experimental work at the Institute of Living in Hartford, Connecticut, it was shown that science's new marvel — the computer — may be able to lend psychiatrists a hand. Scientists at the Institute have developed computer forms that list hundreds of questions designed to characterize the behavior of mental patients during a given day. The nurse in charge checks off appropriate answers to the questions related to a patient's mood (angry, sad, tearful, pleased with himself); appearance (looks tired, worn out, bizarrely dressed); social behavior (quiet, relaxed, fidgety); reaction to medication, activities, etc. At the end of the day such "automatic nurses' notes" are "fed" to the computer, for comparison with the answers to similar *behavior profiles* stored in its "memory." The computer then provides the psychiatrist with a fairly accurate prediction as to the form of drug and psychotherapy from which the individual may be expected to derive the most benefit.

President Kennedy's plea for more basic research into the causes of mental illness is also being heeded. Biochemists are analyzing the blood and urine of mental patients, in the hope of finding unusual metabolic products, as a possible clue that at least some forms of mental deficiency are caused by a chemical malfunctioning of man's complex metabolism.

Of all diseases so investigated, schizophrenia, which affects over 60 per cent of all psychotics, receives the most attention. Indeed, several unusual products have been isolated from the blood or urine of schizophrenic patients.

When injected into laboratory animals, and occasionally into human volunteers, these substances seem to induce schizophrenic behavior of the kind also induced by LSD.

This fact, and the curious chemical resemblance of LSD to several chemical compounds involved in the transmission of nerve impulses, has given support to the hope that schizophrenia is a metabolic disorder like diabetes or PKU, which could perhaps be controlled by drugs or dietary measures.

A better understanding of how the mind functions and develops helps not only the mentally ill, but also sheds light on learning processes. It appears that children have to be taught certain things early if they are to realize their full intellectual potential. Youngsters coming from severely deprived homes, where there is little talk, no toys, no books, no trips to the park — in short, too little personal attention — may never quite catch up with their more privileged age-peers. "Project Head Start," the new school program, especially designed for prekindergarten children, is an attempt at closing this culture gap. Time will tell whether this project remedies the situation.

When Pinel requested permission to treat his patients in a more humane fashion, he was told that he must be mad himself if he wished to unchain such "animals," and for centuries the "alienist," as the psychiatrist was called until recently, was one of the least respected members of the medical profession. It has always been known, however, that psychological factors play an important role in a great many diseases. Conscientious physicians have an "open ear" for their patient's emotional problems, and their possible impact on physical well-being.

Modern mental hospital. Today the Salpêtrière, the largest European hospital complex, combines the very old with the very new.

The twentieth century, however, being an age of specialization, the sympathetic ear of the vanishing family doctor is being replaced by the trained ear of the psychiatrist, who is gradually becoming a member of the general medical team. This seems necessary since, according to the American Hospital Association, about half of all hospitalized patients have emotional problems that contribute to their physical illness. In order to spot such emotional difficulties, some hospitals have psychiatric residents make "rounds" with the general medical team. If necessary, a short session with the psychiatrist is arranged to help a patient become more relaxed before surgery, or enable him to face a new situation with more confidence.

Those who have made psychiatry what it is today came from many different lands and backgrounds. A few set out deliberately to help the mentally ill, but most of them stumbled upon their life's work by accident. Some were doctors by training, others were kind, sensitive human beings moved into action by the suffering of their fellowmen; all were endowed with unusual courage and moral conviction.

That was true of Johann Weyer, who risked burning at the stake for his ideas; of shy Philippe Pinel, who faced one of the most bloodthirsty governments of all times; of argumentative Benjamin Rush; of Dorothea Dix, who forgot her own illness; of wealthy Anton Mesmer; of authoritarian Jean-Martin Charcot; and perhaps most of all, of Sigmund Freud, who, as he said, "dug the tunnel — leaving it to others to provide the light."

In a way, psychiatry can be considered the oldest form of medicine, since in prescientific times a doctor could do little for his patients other than treat them by suggestion, lend them moral support and wait for the healing power of nature. But its real progress was achieved during the last half-century. Today, with the newly discovered psychoactive drugs, and the many different forms of psychotherapy, it is a growing and most exciting branch of medicine.

It still has enormous ground to cover. New, faster, cheaper forms of psychotherapy, suitable for large groups of people, will have to be developed. In spite of recent advances, the wards of the large state institutions are still filled with hopeless, chronically ill patients. Every year thousands of children are born who are, or will be, mentally retarded because of lack of medical care, food, or due to ignorance and neglect.

But a better understanding of man's mental functioning transcends even psychiatry. Medicine and technology, which have provided opportunities for unprecedented health and luxury, have also saddled us with the problems of overpopulation and self-destruction. If mankind is to survive, we will not only have to gain an understanding of our inner selves, but we will have to learn to live peacefully with the three billion souls who share our planet with us.

BIBLIOGRAPHY

BOOKS

Alexander, Franz G. and Selesnick, Sheldon T. *The History of Psychiatry.* New York: Harper and Row, 1966.

Baker, Rachel. *Sigmund Freud.* New York: Julian Messner, 1952.

Breuer, Josef and Freud, Sigmund. *Studies on Hysteria.* New York: Avon Books, 1966.

Freeman, Lucy and Small, Marvin. *The Story of Psychoanalysis.* New York: Pocket Books, 1960.

Freud, Ernst. *Letters of Sigmund Freud.* New York: McGraw-Hill, 1964.

Freud, Martin. *Sigmund Freud: Man and Father.* New York: Vanguard Press, 1958.

Freud, Sigmund. *An Autobiographical Study.* New York: Norton & Co., 1952.

Freud, Sigmund. *The Basic Writings of Sigmund Freud.* New York: Modern Library, 1938.

Gorman, Mike. *Every Other Bed.* Cleveland and New York: The World Publishing Company, 1956.

Guillain, Georges. *J.M. Charcot, His Life, His Work.* New York: Harper & Bros., 1959.

Jones, Ernest. *Life and Work of Sigmund Freud.* New York: Basic Books, 1961.

McKown, Robin. *Pioneers in Mental Health.* New York: Dodd, Mead and Company, 1961.

Riedman, Sarah R. and Green, Clarence C. *Benjamin Rush: Physician, Patriot, Founding Father.* New York: Abelard-Schuman, Ltd., 1964.

Rush, Benjamin. *Medical Inquiries and Observations Upon the Diseases of the Mind.* New York: Hafner Publishing Company, 1962.

Taylor, Norman. *Plant Drugs that Changed the World.* New York: Dodd, Mead and Company, 1965.

Tiffany, Francis. *Life of Dorothea Lynde Dix.* Boston: Houghton, Mifflin and Company, 1891.

Zilboorg, Gregory and Henry, George W. *A History of Medical Psychology.* New York: Norton & Co., 1941.

Zweig, Stefan. *Mental Healers.* Garden City, N.Y.: Garden City Publishing Company, 1934.

PERIODICALS

Harlow, Harry F. "Love in Infant Monkeys," *Scientific American*, (June 1959), 68.
Harlow, Harry F. and Harlow, Margaret Kuenne. "Social Deprivation in Monkeys," *Scientific American*, (November 1962), 136.
Masserman, Jules H. "Experimental Neuroses," *Scientific American*, (March 1950), 38.
Slavson, S.R. "Group Psychotherapy," *Scientific American*, (December 1950), 42.
Wechsberg, Joseph. "Portrait of Hermann Gmeiner," *The New Yorker*, (December 22, 1962), 39.

INDEX

Academy of Science
   Austrian, 96
   French, 80
   German, 52
Aesculapius, 68
Age of Reason, 45
Aggression, 123
Agrippa von Nettesheim, Cornelius, 15
Alkaloid, see reserpine
American Hospital Association, 199
American Psychiatric Association, 38
Anatomy of Melancholy, The, 30-31
Anesthesia, 73
Animal magnetism, 48, 50-51, 65
Animal studies, 148-57
Anna O., 87-92, 104-05, 116
Antidepressants, 170-72, 191
Antihistamines, 169
Antisepsis, 73

Babinski, Joseph, 85
Banting, Frederick, 131
Baquets, 48-50
Bastien and Bastienne, 46
Bedlam, 19, 34
Behavior profiles, 197
Bernard, Claude, 73, 77-78
Bernays, Martha, 97-99, 101
Bernays, Minna, 116
Bernheim, Hippolyte-Marie, 65, 69-72, 82, 89, 103
Best, Charles H., 131
Bicêtre Hospital, 22-24, 26
Biochemistry, 142
Bleuler, Eugen, 116
Bloodletting, 22, 42
Bonaparte, Princess Marie, 124, 126
Bonifacio, Hospital of, 31
Bose, Kartrick Chandra, 164
Braid, James, 65-66, 70
Breuer, Joseph, 87-92, 104-05, 115
British Heart Journal, 166

Bruecke, Ernst, 96, 99, 115
Burghoelzi General Hospital, 117
Burton, Robert, 30-31
Butler, Cyrus, 60
Butler Hospital, 60

Cabot, Dr. Richard C., 177
Case history, 26
Caseworker, 194
Catharsis, 88, 92
Cats, neurotic, 151
Cerletti, Ugo, 127, 134-36
Cervantes, Miguel, 30
Charcot, Jean-Martin, 16, 72-86, 88, 99-102, 104, 115, 127-28, 134, 200
Chevigné, 24
Chiarugi, Vincenzo, 29, 31-32
Chlorpromazine, 171-72
Christ Hospital, 182
Clark University, 117
Cleves, William, Duke of, 16-17
Commons, House of, 32
Commune, 22-23
Community Hospitals
  care of mental patients, 188-95
Complex, 123
Conditioned reflex, 149
Conditioned stimulus, 149
Conflict, 123
Consumption, 175
Cosi fan Tutte, 52
Couthon, Georges, 23

"Dark Ages"
  mental illness, 16
Declaration of Independence, 38
Delusion about Devils, On the, 16

Demoniacs in Art, 84
Diabetes, 131, 140, 177
Diagnostic tests in psychiatry, 195-97
Dickens, Charles, 157
Digitalis, 163
Disease
  emotional factors, 200
Dix, Dorothea Lynde, 54-64, 187, 189, 200
Dix, Elijah, 54-55, 187, 189, 200
Don Quixote, 30
Dream interpretation, 108-09, 112-14
Drug testing in animals, 169-70
Drug therapy, 191, 195

Edinburgh, University of, 37
Ego, 118, 120-21, 123
Ego ideal, 118
Ego and the Mechanisms of Defense, The, 120
Electrodes, 135
Electroshock therapy, 134-36, 168, 191
Elisabeth von R., 105-08, 113, 116
Elliotson, John, 67
Emotional factors in disease, 128, 172, 200
Energizers, 191
Enzymes, 143
Ergotamine, 173
Esdaile, James, 66
EST, *see* Electroshock therapy

Fantasy, 113
Father figure, 123
Fixation, 111
Fliess, Wilhelm, 112, 116
Følling, Ivar Asbjørn, 137-47

Forbidden dreams, 107
Franklin, Benjamin, 21, 37, 50
Free association, 106
French Revolution, 21, 37, 48
Freud, Amalie, 93-94
Freud, Anna, 109, 120
Freud, Jacob, 93
Freud, Martha, 97, 115
Freud, Sigmund, 48, 92-127, 150, 153, 182-83, 200.
  books, 104-05, 117, 124-25
  brain anatomy, 98
  Breuer, 104-05
  Charcot, 99-101, 104
  dream interpretation, 108-09, 112-14
  Goethe prize, 95, 120
  physiology, 96-97
  psychoanalytic movement, 117
  self-analysis, 112
Freudian analysis, 179
Freudian slip, 113-14
Frustration, 169
Functional mental illness, 101

Genetic disorders, 144
Glucose, 132-33
Gmeiner, Hermann, 157-59
Goethe prize, 95, 120
Group therapy, 175-87
  for children, 179
  in the army, 184-85
  types of, 185-86
Guidance counsellors, 195
Guillotin, Dr., 50

Hampstead Child Therapy Clinic, 121
Harlow, Harry F., 152-57
Harlow, Margaret Kuenne, 152-57

Harvard University, 181-82
"Headstart," 198
Hell, Father Maximilian, 46-47
Hellebore, 42, 161-63
High blood pressure, 164-66
Hippocrates, 127-29, 175
Hofmann, Albert, 172-73
Homer, 20
Hunter Bros., 37
Hydrotherapy, 39
Hypertension, 164-66
Hypnotherapy, 184
Hypnotic sleep, 90
Hypnotic suggestion, 103
Hypnotism, 65-72, 102-03
Hysteria, Studies in, 105

Id, 118, 120
Innsbruck, University of, 158
Insane asylums, 32-33, 56-59
Institute for Psychoanalysis, 182
Institute of Children's Diseases, 101
Institute of Living, 197
Institute of Physiology, 96
Insulin, 131
Insulin shock, 132-33, 168
Interpretation of Dreams, The, 114, 117
Iproniazid, 171

Jewish Board of Guardians, 179, 186
Jews, persecution of, 95, 123
Jung, Carl G., 117-18

Kennedy, John F., 187-89, 197
  message, 188-89
Kline, Nathan S., 172

Language of the mind, 108
Latency period, 111
Latin Quarter, 20, 75

Lavoisier, Antoine, 50
Leçons du Mardi, 82, 99
Librium, 172
Lichterfelde Hospital, 131
Liébeault, Ambroise Auguste, 65, 67-72, 82, 89, 103
Lofenalac, 145
Louis XIII, 25
Louis XVI, 21, 48
LSD, 173-74, 198
Lysergic acid diethylamide, 173

Macbeth, 93
Magic Flute, 52
Magnets, 46-48
Maimonides, 130
Malaria, 15, 129, 133
Maria Theresa, Empress, 46, 48
Marie Antoinette, 21, 48
Marie, Pierre, 134
Massachusetts
　General Hospital, 175
　Memorial Hospitals, 166
　State legislature, 57-59
Masserman, Jules, 150-52
Medical Inquiries and Observations Upon the Diseases of the Mind, 39, 43
Melampus, 161-62
Menninger, Charles Frederick, 180
Menninger Clinic, 182-83, 186
Menninger Foundation, 186-87
Menninger, Karl Augustus, 180
Menninger, William Claire, 175, 180-87
Mental deficiency, 39
Mental hospitals
　conditions, 167
Mental illness
　animal studies, 148-57
　biochemistry, 136-47, 197-98
　cost, 188-89
　functional, 101
　incidence, 188, 200
Mental retardation, 39, 137-38, 187-88, 201
　causes, 147
Mesmer, Franz Anton, 44-53, 65-66, 87, 200
Mesmerism, 50-51, 65
Metabolic disorders, 198
Metabolic error, 143
Metabolism, 142-43
Metrazol treatment, 168
Meynert, Theodor, 98
Michelangelo, 121
Middle Ages, 14, 18, 20, 45, 129
Mills, Hannah, 34
Miltown, 172
Minimal brain dysfunction, 196
Monkey raising experiments, 153-57
Monkeys, neurotic, 151
Morphine addiction, 131
Moses, 121, 124-25
Moses and Monotheism, 124-25
Mount Sinai Hospital, 190-95
Mozart, Wolfgang Amadeus, 46, 52-53, 117
Mrs. E., 137

Napoleon III, 79
Narcissistic stage, 110
Narcotherapy, 184
Nervous disorders, 78-79, 178
Neurology, 73, 78, 80
Neuroses, 40, 104, 128, 172
New Jersey
　State Lunatic Asylum, 62, 64
　State legislature, 61-62
New York University, 79
Nichols, John T. G., 56, 58

Northwestern University, 150

Occupational therapy, 42, 192-94
Oedipal stage, 110
Oesterlein, Fräulein Franzl, 47, 87
Orphanage, 157-60

Pappenheimer, Bertha, see Anna O.
Paracelsus, 46
Pasteur, Louis, 73, 80
Pavlov, Ivan Petrovich, 149-50
Pennsylvania Medical College, 38
Peruvian bark, 42
Phenylalanine, 142-43
Phenylalanine-free protein food, 143-44
Phenylketonuria, 137-47, 174, 198
Phenylpyruvic acid, 141-42, 145
Physiology, 73, 149-50
Pietro Leopoldo, Grand Duke of Tuscany, 31
Pinel, Philippe, 13, 19-28, 32, 36, 39, 44-45, 50, 76, 92, 126, 158, 167, 174, 198, 200
Pinel, statue, 76
PKU, see phenylketonuria
Posthypnotic suggestion, 71
Praestigiis Daemonum, De, 16
Pratt, Joseph Hersey, 175-77, 179-80, 185-86
Prentice family, 145-46
Proetus, 161-62
Psychiatric Association, American, 38
Psychiatric services, U.S. Army, 183-85

Psychiatry, clinical, 15
Psychoactive drugs, 191
Psychoanalysis, 88, 105, 108, 191
Psychological response, 149
Psychological testing, 195
Psychopathology of Everyday Life, 117
Psychopharmacology, 161-72, 191
Psychoses, 40-41
Psychostimulant, 170-72
Psychotherapy
 group, 175-87, 191-92
 individual, 192
 occupational, 192-93
 types, 185-86
 use in hospitals, 192
Puységur, Marquis Maxime de, 51-52, 70

Quinine, 42, 163

Rathborn, Mr. & Mrs. William, 56
Rats, neurotic, 170
Rauwolf, Leonhard, 163
Rauwolfia serpentina, 163-69
Redman, Dr. John, 37
Reflex, 149
Repression, 107, 111, 113
Reserpine, 164, 168, 171
Resistance, 106
Response to stimulus, 149
Rhône-Poulenc Laboratories, 169-70, 172
Rockland State Hospital, 172
Roosevelt, Franklin Delano, 124
R.P. 4560, 169-70
Rush, Benjamin, 29, 32, 36-43, 128, 192, 200

Sakel, Manfred, 127, 130-33

St. Luke's Hospital, 34
St. Mary of Bethlehem, Hospital of, 19
Salpêtrière Hospital, 13, 25-26, 28, 75-76, 78-79, 82, 84-85, 99-100, 102, 117, 134, 167
Sancho Panza, 30
Schizophrenia, 41, 132, 168, 174, 189, 197-98
Scribonius Largus, 134
Semelaigne, René, 36
Sen, Gananth, 164
Senile psychosis, 39-40
Sense of guilt, 123
Sexual feelings, infantile, 110
Shakespeare, William, 29-30
Shock therapy, 42, 127-36, 191
Slavson, Samuel R., 175, 178-80, 186
Sleep and Similar States, Examined Especially from the Point of View of the Effect of the Mind on the Body, 69
Snakeroot plant, 163-69
Sorbonne, University of, 20
SOS-Children's Village, 159-60
Sperl Gymnasium, 95
Stimulants, 171-72
Stimulus, 149
Studies in Hysteria, 104-05
Suggestion and Its Application as a Therapy, 69
Superego, 118, 120-21
Surrogate mother, monkey, 153

"Talking Cure," 89
Techlenburg, Countess Anna of, 17

Third Series of Lectures on the Diseases of the Nervous System, 101
Toulouse, University of, 19
Trance state, 70, 103
Tranquilizers, 163-71, 191
Tranquilizing chair, 42
Transference, 92, 111
Trauma, 101
Tuberculosis, 171-72, 175-77
Tuesday lectures, *see Leçons du Mardi*
Tuke, Daniel Hack, 36
Tuke, William, 29, 32, 34-36

Unconditioned reflex, 149
Universitaetsklinik, 133
Uroscopy, 140-41
U.S. Army, psychiatric care in, 182-85

Veterans Administration Hospital, 187
Vienna, General Hospital, 98, 116
University of, 96-97, 131

Wagner-Jauregg, Julius von, 133
Weyer, Johann, 14-28, 200
Wilkins, Robert W., 166
Willis, Thomas, 140
Wisconsin, University of Primate Laboratory, 152, 160
Witches, 14, 16-18
Womb, 81
World War II, 180, 182, 190

York Retreat, 35-36

ALLEN MIDDLE SCHOOL
4225 GETTYSBURG ROAD
CAMP HILL, PA. 17011

DISCARD